BODIES

THE EXHIBITION

People, from time immemorial, have studied and written about the human body. Aristotle, Plato, Hippocrates, Cicero, Galen, Vesalius, Fabricius, Descartes, and Harvey represent a Who's Who of some of the greatest minds who have devoted their talents to this study. And to this list we should not forget to add famous artists like da Vinci, Titian, Michelangelo, Raphael, and Rembrandt, all of whom made significant contributions to our understanding of the human form by combining artistic ability with keen observation.

Why all this interest in the human body? The answer to this question seems quite clear to me: your body is the only thing you carry with you from the moment you are born until your very last breath. Knowledge of one's body, its structure (how it is put together) and its function (how it works) represents some of the most practical, useful information a person could possibly want to possess.

INTRODU

If this is something we can agree on, then how does one explain why so many people today are basically still infants when it comes to an understanding of their own bodies? Too many people abuse their bodies by getting far too little sleep, by eating far too much of the wrong food, by getting far too little exercise, by taking far too many drugs and by drinking far more alcohol than their bodies can tolerate. And, we also know that these abuses carry with them some very significant and serious consequences. It is widely reported in the national press that too many people are overweight, that many preventable medical conditions, such as heart disease and certain forms of cancer, are on the increase and that the already exorbitant costs of medical insurance and hospital care continue to rise. Today it seems that the best medicine anyone could possibly prescribe to get at the root cause of these problems is a good dose of body education.

Just as students who prepare themselves for a career in medicine are required to dissect and study the human body in order to understand its complexities, why can't the average person do much the same thing, if provided with a similar learning experience? This extraordinary Exhibition— *BODIES...THE EXHIBITION*—was designed with that one important purpose in mind: education.

The bodies and organs that you will be looking at are real. Unlike models that idealize the body through the eyes of an artist, the specimens in this Exhibition will show you the body and its parts the way they really are. And, as I've discovered in my more than 30 years of teaching anatomy to medical students, seeing promotes understanding and understanding promotes the most practical kind of body education possible.

How were the specimens in this Exhibition prepared? All of the bodies and organs were preserved using a process called polymer preservation. In this process, tissue water is first removed by submersion in acetone. Then the acetone, too, is removed in a vacuum chamber. During this step in the process, known as impregnation, the tissue spaces within the specimen, formerly filled with acetone, become filled instead with liquid silicone rubber. Lastly, during a step called curing, the silicone rubber is treated with a catalyst and hardened. The end product is a rubberized specimen that can be easily examined without any chance of it

deteriorating due to the natural decay that otherwise would have rendered it unfit for study or public view.

So, in light of all that I've just said, my advice to you is simple. Enjoy your visit to our Exhibition. Join the long list of men and women who throughout the centuries have been amazed by the beauty and the complexity of the human body. Look and be amazed yourself by the complexity of its many bones, muscles, nerves, and blood vessels. Look into the heart, into the brain, into the intestine, into the lungs and leave the exhibition with a greater understanding of how your body works.

Opening yourself to a greater knowledge of your own body will enable you to make more informed decisions about its care and keeping. If you are successful at doing this, then the countless hours of work that have gone into developing and preparing the Exhibition for you to enjoy will have been richly rewarded.

Dr. Roy Glover, Medical Director
Professor Emeritus
Anatomy and Cell Biology
University of Michigan

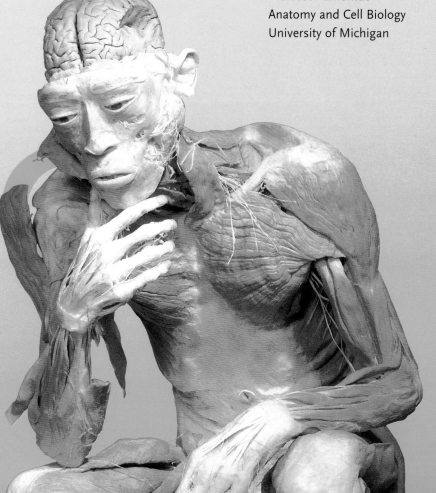

We are all physically unique, from the shade of our skin to the size and shape of our organs. What we have in common is a miraculous set of internal systems, each with its own precise role in how we function. Using authentic human bodies and individual organ specimens, *BODIES... THE EXHIBITION* allows us to look deep inside those systems. What historically was accessible only to the medical profession, is now available for all.

This first full body specimen illustrates the relationship the body's systems have with one another.

SKELETAL SYSTEM

The bones of the skeleton comprise the body's supporting internal framework. This specimen reveals the types of bone that make up the human body: long bones (arms, forearms, thighs, and legs); flat bones (sternum, scapula, and skull); short bones (wrists and ankles); irregular bones (vertebrae); and sesamoid bones (kneecap).

MUSCULAR SYSTEM

Muscles give the body much of its individual shape and generate heat to help maintain its optimal temperature. When a muscle contracts it shortens, pulling bones together, causing movement at the joint it crosses. For example, the biceps brachii muscle of the arm crosses joints at the shoulder and the elbow. Its contraction can cause movement at one or both of these joints.

NERVOUS SYSTEM

Nerve impulses travel to and from the surface of the body along microscopic nerve fibers. Thousands of these fibers are collected together within a peripheral nerve. This arrangement is very similar to the bundle of individual fibers found within a fiber optic telephone cable that carries multiple conversations in many directions.

Tough white peripheral nerves are clearly visible in the upper and lower limbs of this specimen, while a more delicate network of nerves can be seen in the cheek.

DIGESTIVE SYSTEM

The length of the digestive tract illustrates the importance of our digestive systems. More than twenty feet long, our digestive tracts convert the food we eat into the fuel our bodies need. Once converted, it is absorbed through the wall of the tract and carried by the bloodstream throughout the body to reach and nourish the cells that perform all of the body's vital functions.

RESPIRATORY SYSTEM

The lungs resemble a soft sponge that expands with each breath. When you inhale, air enters the lungs filling the three hundred million or more alveoli (air sacs) at the ends of the airways. In the alveoli, oxygen from the outside air is absorbed into the body and exchanged for carbon dioxide, which is then exhaled. The absorbed oxygen is then transported via the blood to every cell of the body.

CIRCULATORY SYSTEM

The circulatory system is made up of the heart and thousands of miles of blood vessels. One of the largest of these blood vessels, the aorta and its branches, supplies oxygenated blood to every part of the body. Two major arteries on either side of the neck (the right and left common carotid arteries) supply the brain. These are the arteries pressed when taking your pulse.

REPRODUCTIVE SYSTEM

The testes produce the male sex cell, the sperm; the ovaries produce the female sex cell, the ova. When the sperm and ova join, a process known as fertilization occurs.

URINARY SYSTEM

This system includes the ureters, the bladder, the urethra, and the primary organs of the system—two kidneys. The kidneys lie within the abdominal cavity where they are slightly offset because of the location of the liver. The right kidney lies a bit lower in the abdomen than the left. They produce urine, the fluid by which the body rids itself of its harmful waste material, which is then stored in the bladder until eliminated through the urethra. The urinary bladder, surrounded by the pelvic bones, can store more than 1.5 pints (over 600 milliliters) of urine before needing to be emptied.

INTEGUMENT SYSTEM

This system is made up of the skin and its major appendages, the sweat glands, hair, and nails. The skin is the largest and heaviest organ of the body. It functions in many different ways: as a sensory receptor, as a protector of the tissues beneath it, and as a regulator of body temperature. In addition, the skin contains a series of genetically determined ridges that are responsible for our fingerprints.

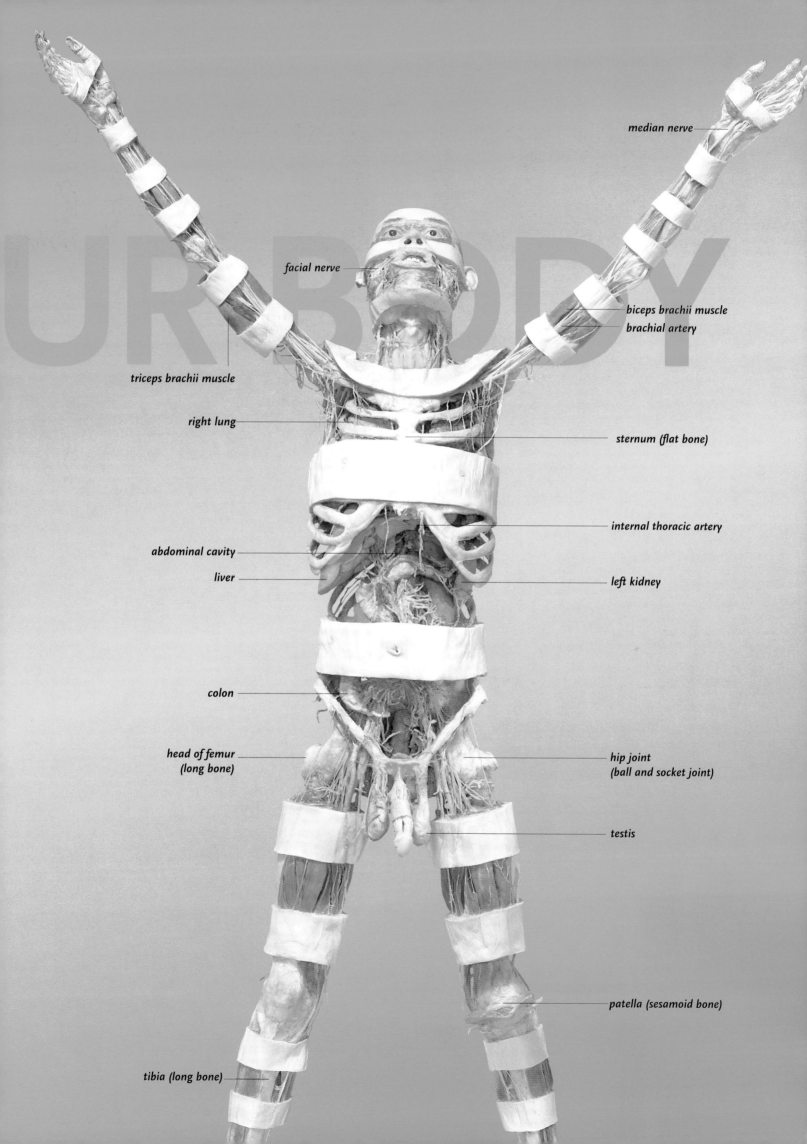

median nerve

facial nerve

biceps brachii muscle

brachial artery

triceps brachii muscle

right lung

sternum (flat bone)

internal thoracic artery

abdominal cavity

liver

left kidney

colon

head of femur
(long bone)

hip joint
(ball and socket joint)

testis

patella (sesamoid bone)

tibia (long bone)

SKELETAL

O f all the anatomical structures beneath our skins, we are most familiar with our skeletons. They are the subject of myth and legend and remain a visual reminder of our humanity long after our softer tissues have disappeared. Like the framework of a house, skeletons form the internal structure of the body, permitting us to resist the force of gravity, move through space, and carry our skins with dignity. They are a perfect combination of form and function: the S-shaped spine keeps the body upright and supports the head, while the pelvis balances the upper body over the feet.

Male and female skeletons are similar in nature. However, the female frame is usually lighter and smaller than the male frame, and includes a wider pelvis for childbirth. Somewhat delicate in appearance, the bones in our skeletal system are actually four to five times stronger than steel, but make up only 14 percent of the body's total weight.

The skeleton derives its name from the Greek *skeletos*, which means dry. But the bones of the human skeleton are anything but dry; they are dynamic organisms that reinvent themselves in response to repeated stress and repair themselves when broken.

BONES OF THE HAND AND WRIST

The association of the bones and ligaments in the wrist and hand allows for great mobility and dexterity. Evolution has freed our upper limbs from the burden of bearing weight and locomotion, enabling us to grasp objects and manipulate them with precision.

SYSTEM

Made up of approximately 206 bones, our skeletons have multiple functions:

They protect our internal organs.

They store the calcium and phosphorus necessary for their own strength and flexibility, and for proper nerve and muscle function.

They serve as anchors for our muscles, forming a team that gives the body action.

The marrow inside the flat bones and long bones of the adult skeletal system creates 2.5 million new red blood cells each second, facilitating the transfer of oxygen from our lungs to our tissues.

BONES AND JOINTS

Visible on this specimen are the bones and joints of the body. Joints, or articulations, are the areas where our bones meet. They are classified by the range of movement they allow. For example, hinge joints (elbows, knees, fingers, and toes) allow the bones to swing in two directions. Ball and socket joints (hips and shoulder) allow some rotation, as well as movement back and forth, and from side to side. Pivot joints facilitate a left to right movement similar to the course your head takes as it swivels on your spine.

humerus
(arm
long bone)

shoulder
(ball and socket joint)

rib cartilage

elbow
(hinge joint)

intervertebral disc

sacrum

bony pelvis

carpal bones
(wrist,
gliding joint)

phalanges

femur
(thigh long bone)

patella
(sesamoid bone)

fibula
(small shinbone)

tibia
(large shinbone)

tarsal bones
(ankle gliding joint)

metatarsals

BONES, MUSCLE, AND CARTILAGE

This dissection demonstrates the important relationship between the bones of our skeletons and the cartilage and muscle attached to these bones.

Cartilage is a tough and flexible connective tissue that allows bones to slide over one another at all moveable joints, reducing friction, and preventing damage. If cartilage breaks down in the knees, pain and bone damage may result. Weakened cartilage in one of the back's vertebra might lead to a slipped or crushed vertebral disc.

Lighter and more flexible than bone, cartilage strengthens non weight-bearing parts of the body, such as the nose and outer ears. Bend your ear toward your face and notice that it instantly regains its original shape when released. The elasticity of cartilage makes this possible.

Muscle and bone flow seamlessly together at every intersection of the body. Observe the areas surrounding the joints on this specimen and the muscles that work in tandem with them:

The *biceps brachii muscle*, as its name implies, consists of two heads. One head originates from the scapula, while the second head arises from the humerus (upper arm bone). Both heads insert into the radius bone of the forearm via a common tendon. The biceps brachii muscle helps us to flex both the arm and the forearm and also acts to turn our palms upward (supination) when the forearm is flexed.

The *pronator teres muscle* crosses the right elbow joint and attaches to the radius bone. It allows us to turn our hands palm down.

The *intercostal muscles* located between the ribs are essential for breathing. Their contractions raise and lower the rib cage, providing room for the lungs as they expand and contract with each breath.

The *quadratus lumborum muscles*, wide bands of muscles that connect the lower back to the hip, help us to bend our backs from side to side and to force air out of our lungs.

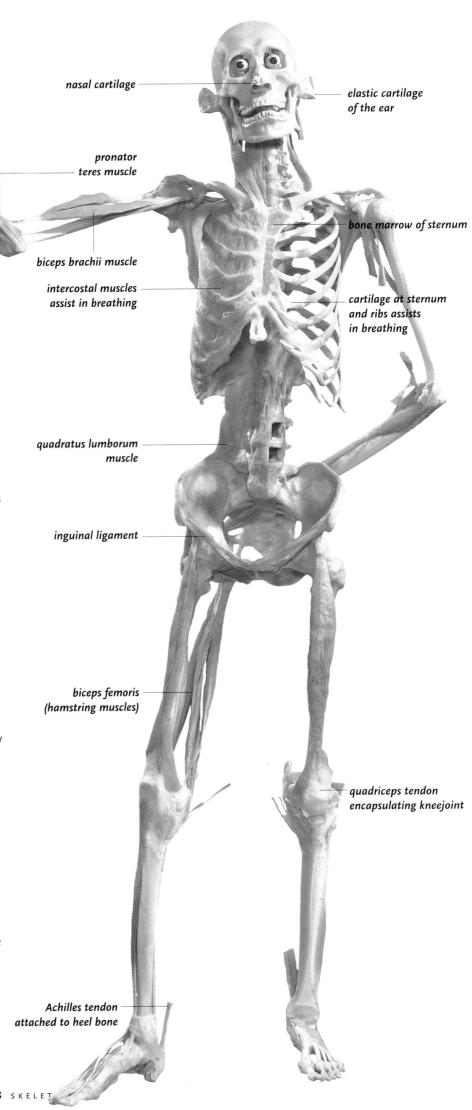

nasal cartilage

elastic cartilage of the ear

pronator teres muscle

bone marrow of sternum

biceps brachii muscle

intercostal muscles assist in breathing

cartilage at sternum and ribs assists in breathing

quadratus lumborum muscle

inguinal ligament

biceps femoris (hamstring muscles)

quadriceps tendon encapsulating kneejoint

Achilles tendon attached to heel bone

The *biceps femoris*, one of the hamstring muscles, is visible on the back of the thigh. It assists in extending the thigh and in flexing and rotating the leg. Pulled hamstring muscles are common in athletes who perform quick starts and stops.

KNEE JOINT AND ITS BONES

This is the largest and most complex joint in the body—as well as the weakest and most vulnerable to injury. Primarily a hinge joint, it is also capable of some rotational movement. The knee is formed where the rounded end of the femur (thighbone) meets the flattened end of the tibia (shinbone of the leg). The third bone of the knee, the patella (kneecap), is embedded within the tendon of the powerful quadriceps femoris muscle of the thigh. The kneecap protects the knee and increases leverage of the quadriceps muscle.

HIP JOINT

One of the strongest and most stable joints in the body, the hip joint (a ball and socket joint), is formed where the ball at the head of the femur fits into the acetabulum (socket) of the hipbone. This flexible joint structure allows for rotation, movement forward, backward, and from side to side. Held in place by five ligaments, as well as tough connective tissue deep in the joint, the hip joint is often called upon to withstand 400 pounds of force in everyday activity.

ELBOW JOINT

Formed by three bones, three ligaments, and fourteen muscles, the elbow joint permits flexion, extension, and rotation of the forearm. This dissection clearly shows the articular cartilage at the end of the humerus, where it widens to accept the radius and ulna of the forearm to form the elbow joint.

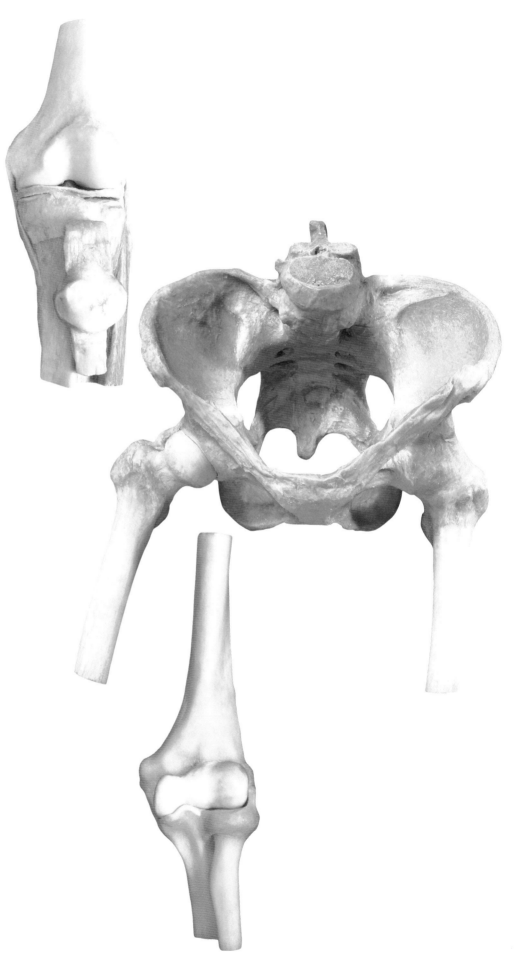

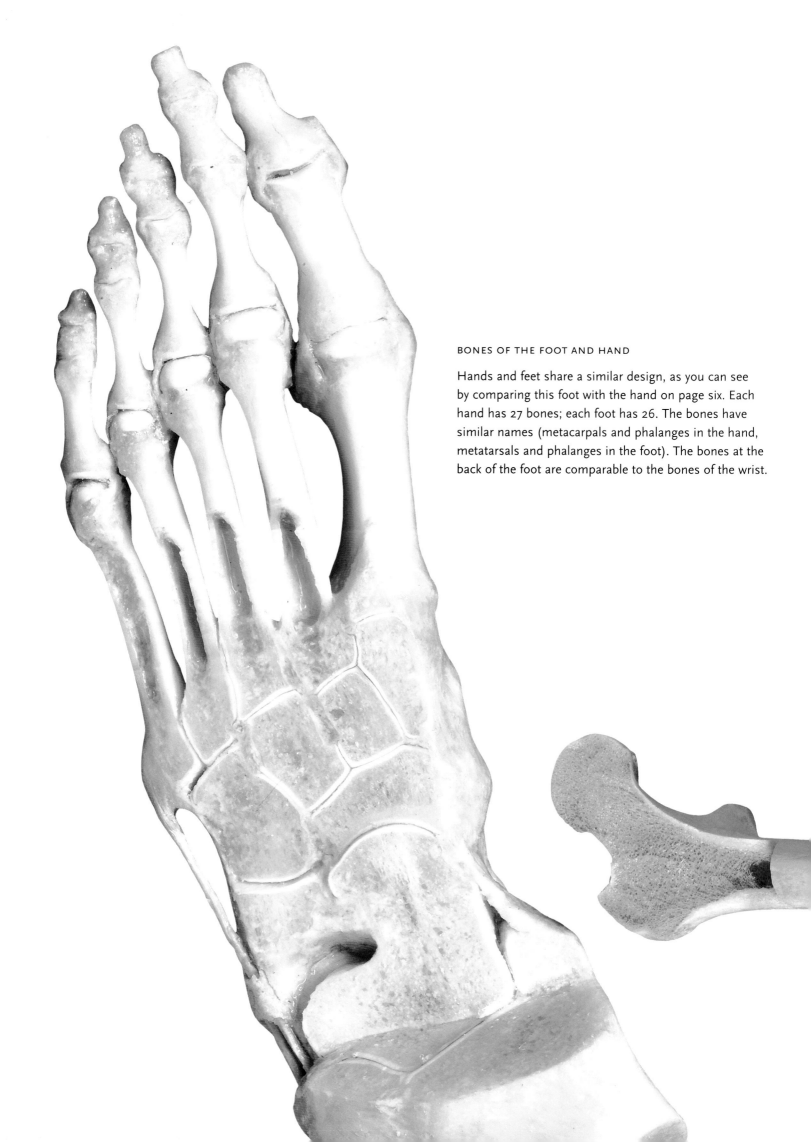

BONES OF THE FOOT AND HAND

Hands and feet share a similar design, as you can see by comparing this foot with the hand on page six. Each hand has 27 bones; each foot has 26. The bones have similar names (metacarpals and phalanges in the hand, metatarsals and phalanges in the foot). The bones at the back of the foot are comparable to the bones of the wrist.

CROSS SECTION OF FEMUR

The bones of the body are made of two types of bone tissue: spongy bone and compact bone. Spongy bone, found at the ends of long bones, such as the femur (thighbone) shown below, is composed of tiny bone spurs called trabeculae. They are arranged along the lines of greatest stress and pressure. This organization allows bones to be light and yet support the greatest amount of weight. Compact bone makes up the outer layer of most bones, particularly the long bones. Its dense organization provides bones with the strength necessary to resist everyday compressive forces.

Bone growth in the long bones of children and young adults progresses as bone cells are replaced by cartilage. Growth plates, made of hyaline cartilage, lie near each end of a long bone. During bone growth, bone cells work to break down this cartilage, replacing it with more bone. As long as the cartilage disc grows faster than bone cells can replace it, bone growth continues. Even after growth stops, bone is constantly regenerating as specialized bone cells create new bone, while other cells remove older bone.

The shafts of the long bones are hollow and contain a soft substance known as marrow. Red bone marrow manufactures most of our red blood cells, which then carry oxygen throughout the body. In addition, the marrow also produces white blood cells that protect the body from invading bacteria and viruses.

MAXILLA

The paired maxillary bones form the upper jaw. They connect with every bone of the face with the exception of the lower jaw. The maxillary bones help to form the eye sockets, or orbits, and also contain the maxillary sinuses, the largest sinuses found in the head. The sinuses are cavities within the skull that make it lighter and give resonance to the voice.

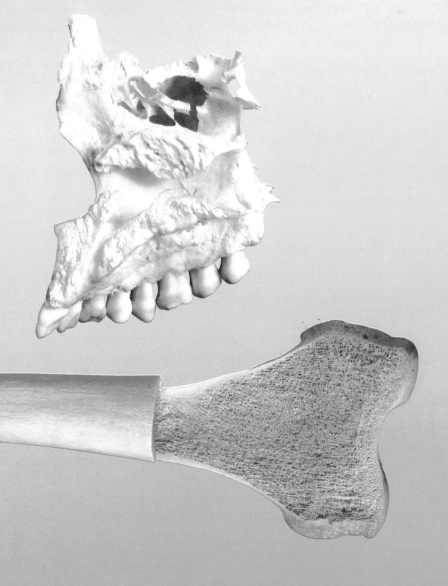

VERTEBRAL COLUMN

The vertebral column, or spine, typically consists of 33 vertebrae, which support and stabilize the upper body while forming a strong and flexible housing for the spinal cord. In addition, the spine has four natural curves that help it distribute weight and absorb shock.

Vertebrae increase in size as they progress down the spine.

The vertebrae that make up the spine include:

Cervical   The cervical vertebrae are the least robust of the vertebrae yet they are strong enough to support the neck and at the same time allow for its rather wide range of motion. The first two cervical vertebrae, the atlas and axis, allow for complex rotational movements of the head.

Thoracic   These twelve vertebrae are slightly larger than the cervical vertebrae. Each has a facet, which connects with the head of each of the twelve ribs.

Lumbar   The five lumbar vertebrae are the largest and strongest of all the vertebrae. They bear the greatest amount of weight and thus provide the greatest amount of support.

Sacrum   The sacrum is composed of five fused vertebrae. These vertebrae help form the bony pelvis and articulate with the coccyx or tailbone.

COCCYX

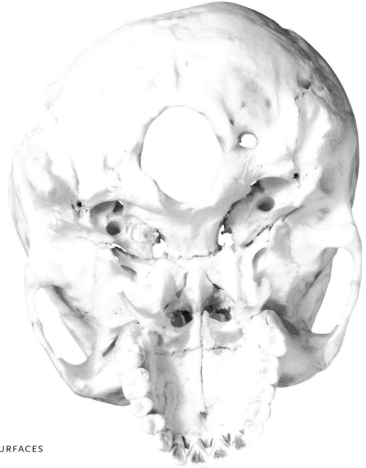

EXTERNAL AND INTERNAL SURFACES OF THE SKULL

These unusual views of the skull allow you to see the complex composition of bone at the base of the skull and the several openings (foramina) that allow blood vessels and nerves to pass into and out of the cranial cavity. The largest of these openings, the foramen magnum, is the point at which the spinal cord connects with the brain. Notice also the zygomatic (cheek) arches on either side of the skull; they provide the bony foundation for the cheeks and are points of attachment for some of the muscles of mastication and facial expression.

Our skulls include the smallest bones in our bodies. Called auditory ossicles (hearing bones), they are located within the temporal bones of the skull and have distinct shapes for which they are named. They are the malleus (hammer), the incus (anvil), and the stapes (stirrup). Connected by the smallest movable joints in the body, these bones transfer sound vibrations from the surface of the eardrum to the delicate oval window of the inner ear. Because the eardrum is much larger than the oval window, even the smallest vibration of the eardrum results in a significant vibration of the oval window. This allows us to hear even the faintest whisper.

AUDITORY OSSICLES

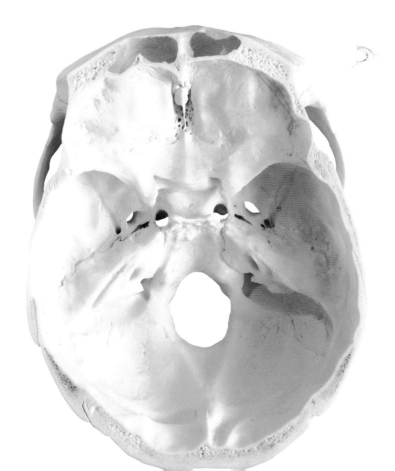

SKULL
INTERNAL SURFACE

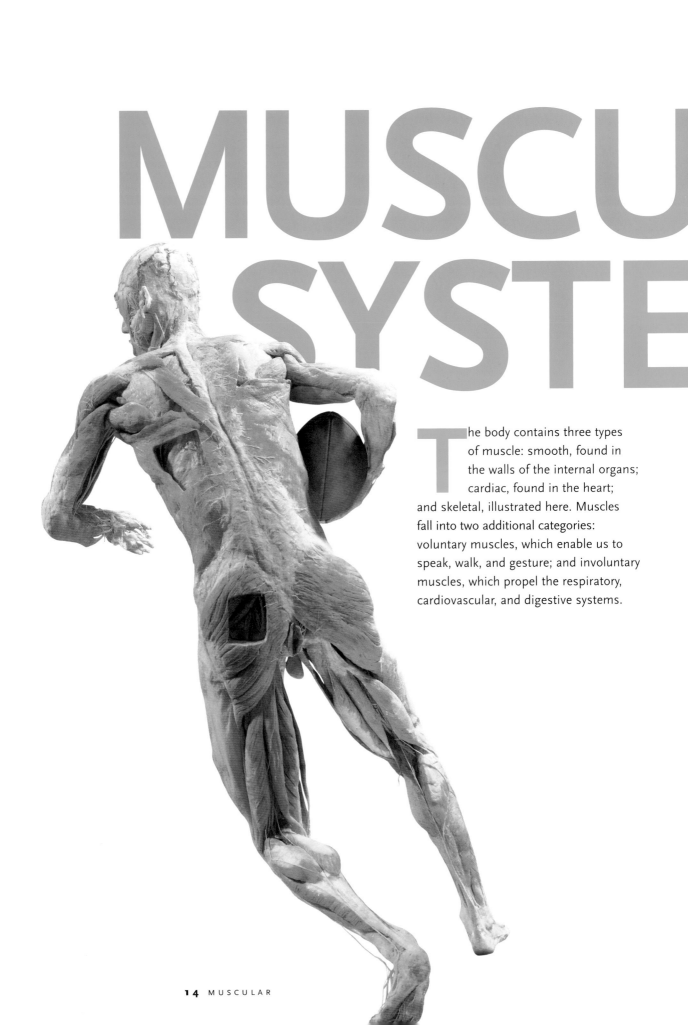

MUSCU
SYSTE

The body contains three types of muscle: smooth, found in the walls of the internal organs; cardiac, found in the heart; and skeletal, illustrated here. Muscles fall into two additional categories: voluntary muscles, which enable us to speak, walk, and gesture; and involuntary muscles, which propel the respiratory, cardiovascular, and digestive systems.

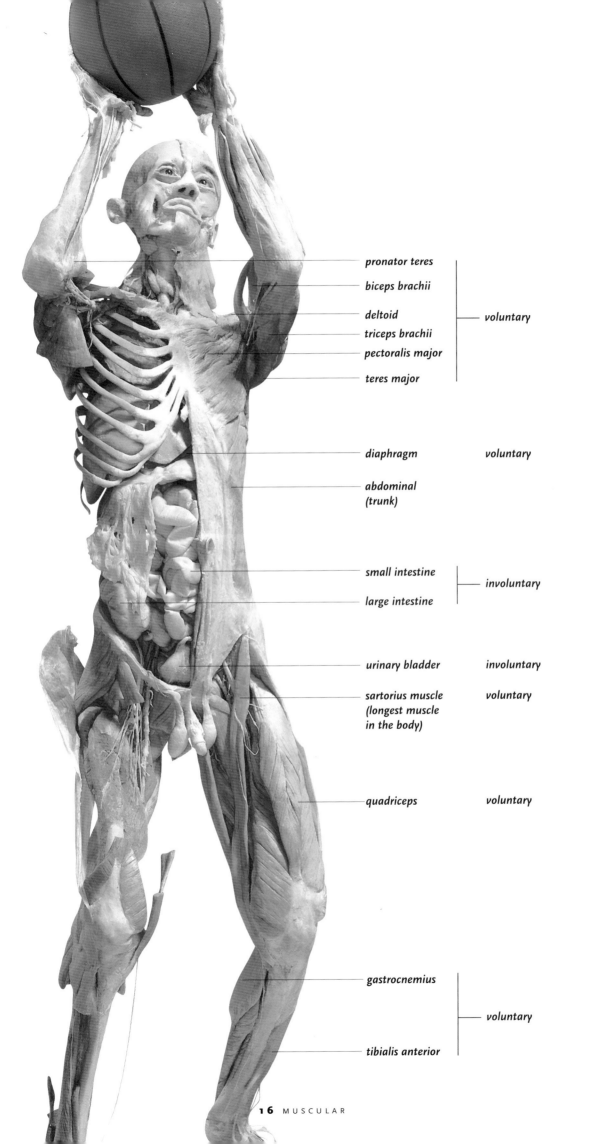

pronator teres

biceps brachii

deltoid

triceps brachii

pectoralis major

teres major

voluntary

diaphragm — voluntary

abdominal
(trunk)

small intestine

large intestine

involuntary

urinary bladder — involuntary

sartorius muscle
(longest muscle
in the body) — voluntary

quadriceps — voluntary

gastrocnemius

tibialis anterior

voluntary

SKELETAL MUSCLES (VOLUNTARY)

The skeletal muscles are by far the largest group of muscles. More than six hundred of them line and wrap nearly every square inch of our body. They make up approximately 23 percent of a female's body weight and 40 percent of a male's, and are the muscles that account for much of our physical form. They also provide:

Movement and posture A level of continual contraction, called muscle tone, is the force that keeps us upright and ready for action, despite gravity.

Protection Four layers of skeletal muscles that connect at the ribcage and pelvic bones protect the internal organs of the abdomen.

Body Heat Through their contractions and cellular respiration, skeletal muscles play an important role in homeostasis, the maintenance of the body's constant temperature at 98.6°F (37°C). If the hypothalamus, the heat-promoting center in the brain, detects a drop in body temperature, it signals the muscles and we shiver. This increase in muscular activity produces heat, which raises the body's temperature.

The dynamic pose of the specimen opposite illustrates the body's skeletal muscle groups working together to achieve remarkable agility and balance.

WORKING TOGETHER

Every bodily movement requires several muscles working together to initiate, assist and control motion. The prime mover carries out the major action, while synergist muscles contract with the prime mover to assist in that action. Antagonist or relaxed muscles, however, do not contract, which allows the prime mover to complete its action.

In the complicated movement of shooting a basketball, three prime movers are involved: the deltoid at the shoulder, the biceps brachii at the elbow, and the pronator teres at the forearm. The corresponding antagonists are the teres major, the triceps brachii, and the supinator.

MOTOR UNITS

Muscles are made up of motor units, a specific group of muscles cells controlled by one nerve cell. The finer the motion, the smaller the motor unit; more powerful motions require larger motor units. The motor unit that moves the tip of your little finger contains far fewer muscles than those that kick your leg.

CORE MUSCLES

This specimen also illustrates how important the abdominal muscles are to motion and control. The abdominal muscles form the center of the body, connecting to both the muscles of the lower limbs, upper limbs, and back. Weak abdominal muscles can lead to injuries throughout the skeletal muscular system.

INVOLUNTARY MUSCLES

While voluntary muscles, such as the skeletal muscles, are under your control, the involuntary smooth muscles of the body work without any direction from you. For that reason, they often go unnoticed.

These muscles are essential in all of our major body systems and are responsible for such vital functions as the amount of air that enters our lungs, the rate at which our hearts beat, and the speed at which the food we eat travels though our digestive tracts.

It has been suggested that if all the muscles in the body worked together, they would generate enough power to lift more than ten tons.

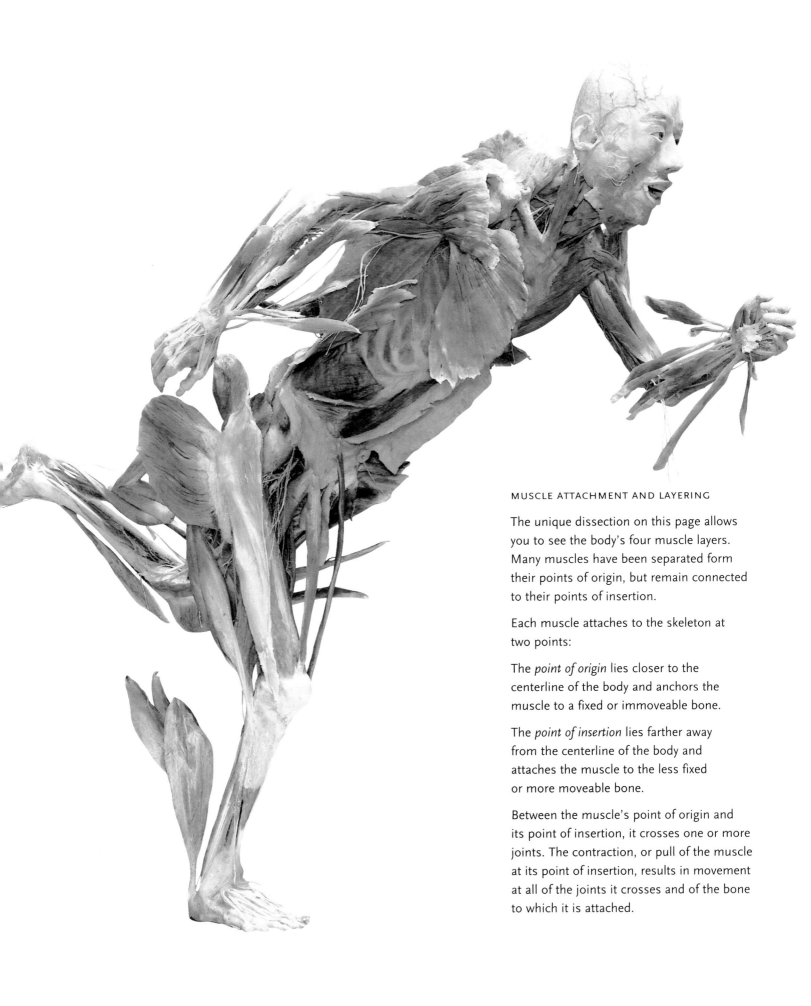

MUSCLE ATTACHMENT AND LAYERING

The unique dissection on this page allows you to see the body's four muscle layers. Many muscles have been separated form their points of origin, but remain connected to their points of insertion.

Each muscle attaches to the skeleton at two points:

The *point of origin* lies closer to the centerline of the body and anchors the muscle to a fixed or immoveable bone.

The *point of insertion* lies farther away from the centerline of the body and attaches the muscle to the less fixed or more moveable bone.

Between the muscle's point of origin and its point of insertion, it crosses one or more joints. The contraction, or pull of the muscle at its point of insertion, results in movement at all of the joints it crosses and of the bone to which it is attached.

MUSCLES OF THE ANKLE AND FOOT

The arrangement of the muscles and ligaments of the foot, along with the bones to which they attach, provide support and stability for the foot and distribute the body's weight over a broad area. All of the above are essential for the arched sole of your foot. Arches allow the foot to move properly, absorb shock, and cushion the pressure of several thousand pounds per square inch every time we take a step. In addition, they protect the integrity of the blood vessels and nerves of the foot by keeping them from being crushed when we walk.

GLUTEAL MUSCLES AND ILIOTIBIAL TRACT

The gluteus maximus muscle was named after the Greek word for "bottom" and is one of the largest and most powerful muscles of the body. All three layers of gluteal muscle, the gluteus maximus, medius, and minimus, are visible on the above specimen. They sit one on top of the other, each named according to its depth. These three muscles act together to extend, abduct, and rotate the thigh when walking. As you may know from past experience, the gluteus maximus often serve as the site of intramuscular injections.

The connective tissue sheath seen running beside the gluteus muscle is called the iliotibial tract. It runs between the hipbone (ileum) and the shinbone (tibia) on the outside of your leg. It helps prevent the knee from buckling during walking while the other foot is off the ground.

PECTORALIS MUSCLES

Both the pectoralis major and minor muscles are visible on the specimen below. The larger pectoralis major muscles lie on top of the pectoralis minor on both sides of the chest and act to move your arm across your chest.

The pectoralis minor runs diagonally between the chest and shoulder. It is one of five muscles used when you lift your shoulder blade to move your arm back as you would in a golf swing. Because it is not a prime mover, but only assists in this action, the pectoralis minor is a synergist muscle.

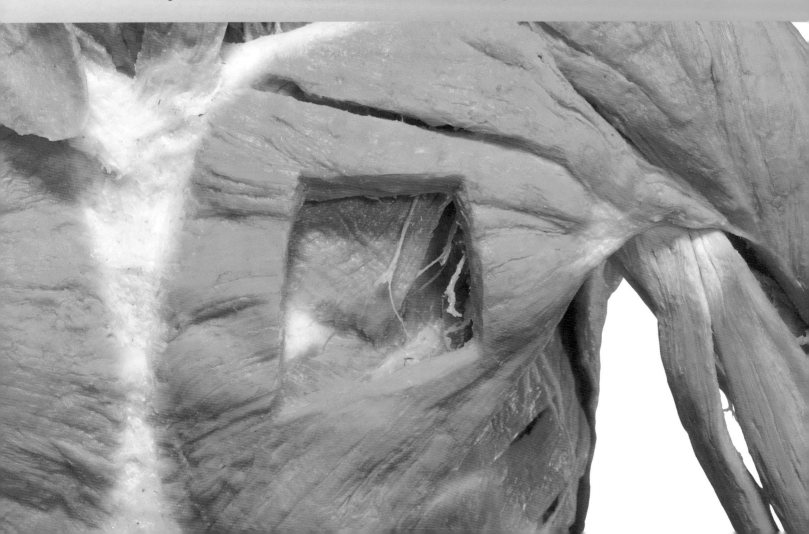

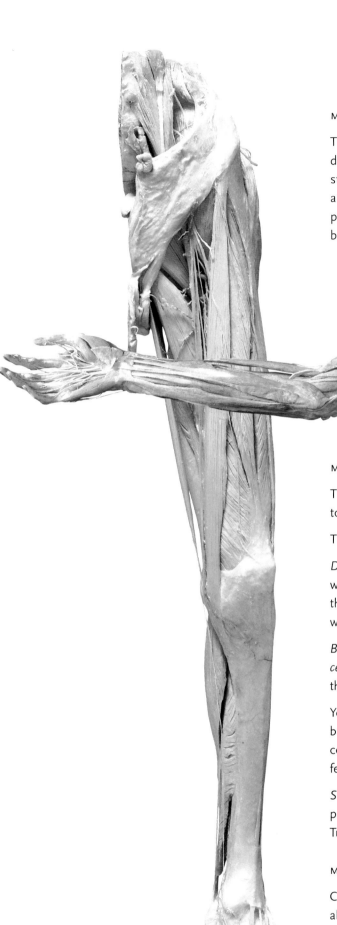

MUSCLES OF THE ARM AND LEG

The muscles of the arm and leg share similar designs, but perform different functions. The larger muscles of the leg must support and stabilize the body. The muscles of the arm are not required to bear weight and are free to perform finer tasks. However, both of these muscle groups possess strength and agility. The arm can develop the power to shoot a basket and the leg can be trained to execute a graceful pose.

MUSCLES OF THE UPPER LIMB

The numerous muscles of the upper limb constantly work together to perform tasks such as writing, lifting, and sipping coffee.

These muscles include:

Deltoid The deltoid muscle, which joins the upper arm to the shoulder, was named for its shape, that of a triangle, *delta* in Greek. It serves to lift the arm away from the side of the body, as well as allowing forward, backward, and side-to-side movement.

Biceps The word *biceps* comes from two Latin words: *bi*, meaning two; and *cephalon*, meaning head. The biceps muscle has two heads, a long head that attaches to the scapula and a short head that attaches to the humerus.

You actually have two sets of biceps muscles, the biceps brachii and the biceps femoris. In each case, their complete name designates both their common shape (two heads) and their specific location (brachii—arm; femoris—thigh).

Supinator and Pronator These two muscles are named for the actions they perform. Turn your palm upward—that is the supinator muscle working. Turn your palm down—that is the pronator at work.

MUSCLES OF THE LOWER LIMB

Containing the largest muscles in the body, the muscles of the lower limb allow us to be bipedal and mobile. They include:

Sartorius This muscle is the longest in the body. Its takes its name from the Latin word *sartor,* meaning "mender," relating to the position in which tailors often sit when they sew—with one leg crossed over the other— a position this muscle allows.

Quadriceps This four-headed muscle makes up most of the muscle mass on the front and outside of the thigh and joins into the powerful patellar tendon just above the knee.

NERVOUS

The brain and the spinal cord make up the central nervous system. All the nerves that branch from the brain and the spinal cord are known as the peripheral nervous system. Together, these two systems, the most complex in your body, act as both your chief executive and chief operating officer.

The peripheral nervous system continually updates the central nervous system, sending information via sensory nerves to the brain, where more than 12 billion nerve cells process that information. Once brain cells have determined the appropriate response to a stimulus, they send commands back to the body through motor nerves.

SPINAL CORD

As the main conduit between the brain and the body, the spinal cord transmits millions of nerve impulses per second at speeds exceeding 270 miles per hour.

Signals brought to the spinal cord via sensory nerves from all over the body travel up the spinal cord (about the width of your little finger) to higher centers of the brain where we become aware (conscious) of them. In other cases, we react to sensory signals carried to the spinal cord without any conscious awareness of them. This non-thinking type of reaction is known as a reflex. Think of the instantaneous response that occurs when you pull your hand away from something hot.

As soon as the spinal cord receives a distressed nerve impulse, it commands the endangered part of the body to move. Such reflex responses are predictable (they do not change from person to person) and serve to protect the body from injury.

The adult spinal cord is roughly 18–19 inches (approximately 45 centimeters) long. In the fetus, the spinal cord extends all the way down to the coccyx or tailbone. But as development proceeds, the spinal cord is drawn upward so that in most adults it ends at a point just above the hips.

With the protective meninges removed from the specimen at right, the tapered end of the spinal cord is easily visible. Also visible on the lower section of the spinal cord is the cauda equina, the collection of lumbar and sacral spinal nerve roots thought to resemble the tail of a horse. Since the lower region of the vertebral canal does not contain the spinal cord, cerebrospinal fluid can be recovered from this space via a long hypodermic needle inserted between the lower lumbar vertebrae. This spinal tap allows physicians to examine the cerebrospinal fluid to diagnose conditions of the nervous system.

SPINAL NERVES

Thirty-one pairs of peripheral nerves carry messages to and from the spinal cord. These nerves are named for the region of the spine from which they emerge: cervical, thoracic, lumbar, sacral, and coccygeal. Spinal nerves emerge from between our vertebrae and then branch out to supply the skin and muscles of the neck, trunk, and limbs as well as many of our internal organs. Nerves become finer and finer the closer they come to the body's surface.

The spinal nerves along with the cranial nerves, which arise directly from the brain, are the main lines of communication between the body and the central nervous system. They provide the brain and spinal cord with necessary information about what is happening in the body so they, in turn, can make the decisions necessary to keep us safe and healthy.

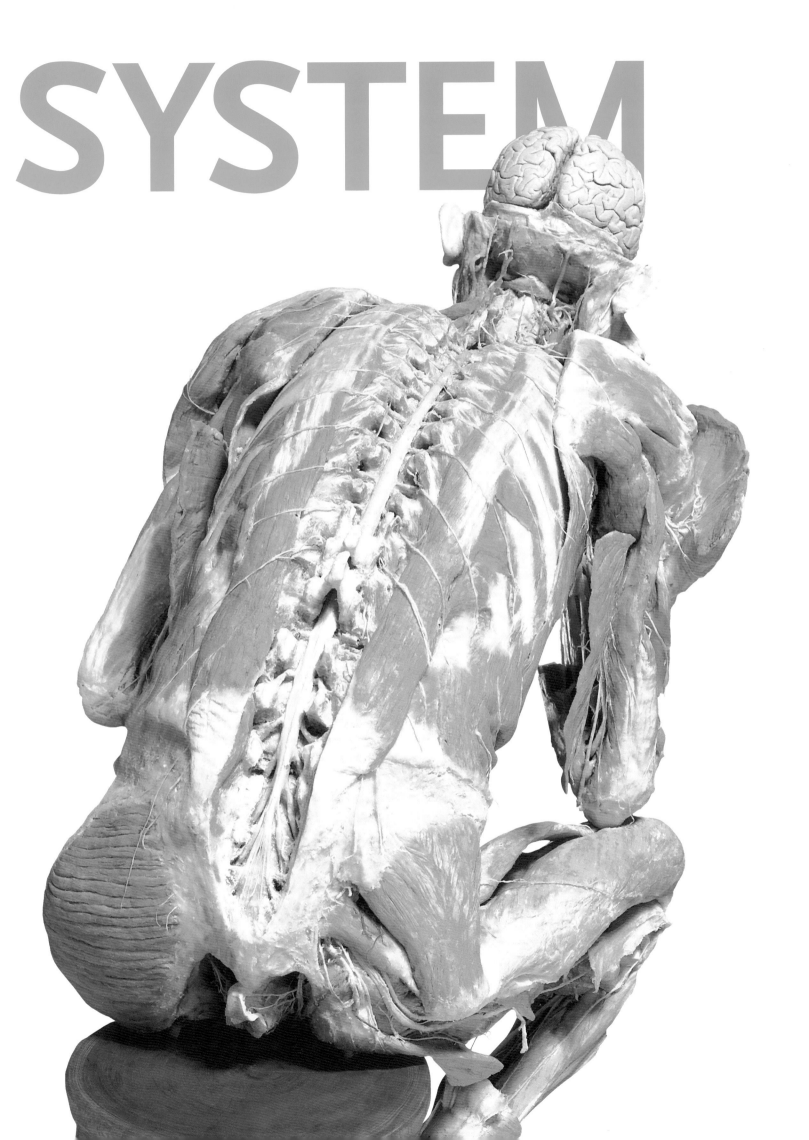

SYSTEM

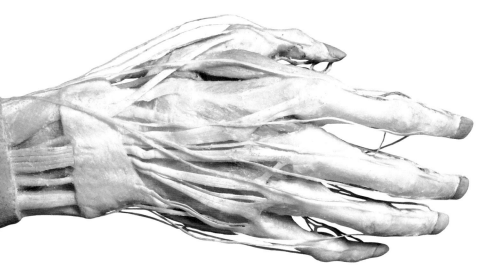

NERVES OF THE HAND

The nerves that innervate the hand include both motor and sensory nerve fibers. Motor nerve fibers carry information from the spinal cord to the muscles of the hand, causing the fingers to move. Sensory nerve fibers carry information from the hand back to the spinal cord. Sensory nerves monitor everything from the stretch of muscles and joints, to blood pressure in the blood vessels.

CRANIAL NERVES

Twelve pairs of peripheral nerves attach to the brain. These nerves primarily transmit impulses to and from structures in the head, including the eyes, the teeth, and the muscles of the face. Cranial nerves also carry information related to smell, taste, sight, sound, and balance back to the brain.

BODILY CONTROL AND CREATIVITY

The specimen at right illustrates the nearly countless number of tasks the brain executes, from the most basic to the highly complex. It monitors our internal organs without our awareness; it oversees the rate at which we grow; and it moves our limbs when we command. At the same time, our brain also gives rise to all of our creative efforts and our will to perform them, from visual art to math to conducting a symphony.

AUTOMOMIC NERVES AND NERVE PLEXUSES

Many peripheral nerves are visible on this specimen. These include the nerves innervating the upper and lower limbs, as well as the nerves supplying organs deep within the body cavities. The nerves traveling to the internal organs are collectively referred to as visceral nerves. They provide autonomic (involuntary) impulses to all our internal organs, including the heart, lungs, digestive, and reproductive organs.

Autonomic nerves also help regulate the body's fight or flight responses when we perceive danger or are under increased stress; blood flow is diverted from the skin to the organs, increasing our ability to take action, but leaving us with that cold clammy feeling.

This specimen also reveals the dense webs where many peripheral nerves come together. Each of these webs, known as a nerve plexus, is a site where thousands of nerve fibers intermingle before branching into the limbs or viscera. The brachial plexuses are visible in the armpits of this specimen; the lumbosacral plexuses are located close to the hips; and the solar plexus is exposed in the center of the abdomen.

No nerve entering a plexus is the same when it exits. Because of the plexuses' intricate makeup, we cannot understand them by looking; a knowledge of fetal nerve development is necessary.

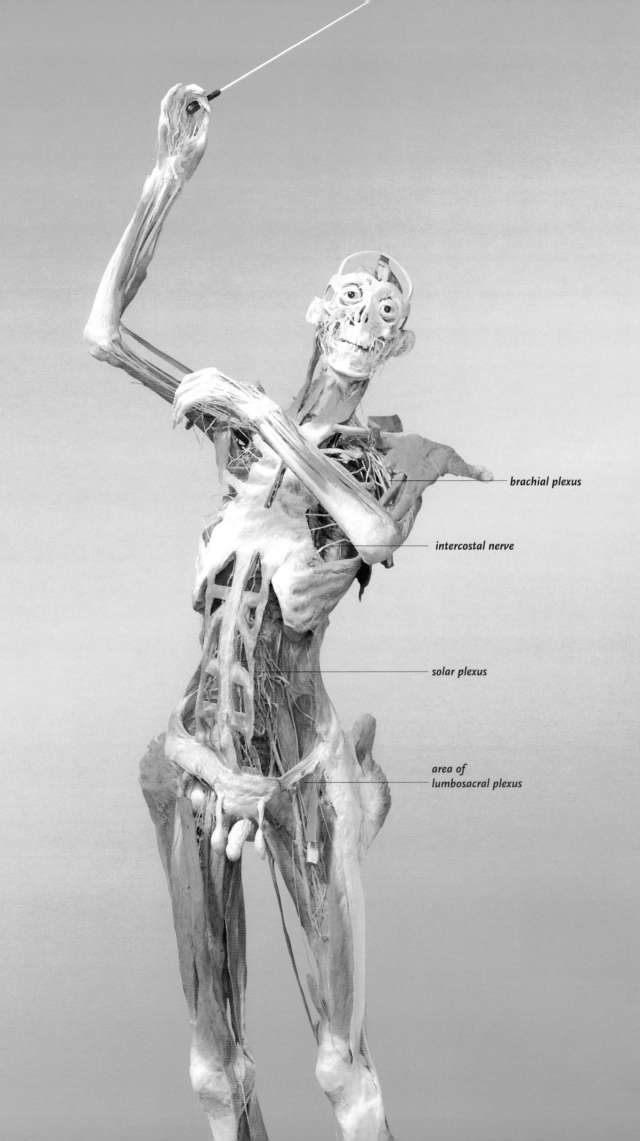

brachial plexus

intercostal nerve

solar plexus

area of
lumbosacral plexus

NERVE PATHWAYS

This specimen's dissection exposes the intricate nerves of the face, as well as those nerves that control digestion and respiration.

The network of facial nerves visible on the left side of the face are colloquially referred to as the "duck's foot" because of their wide, webbed structure. These nerves activate the organs and muscles of the face. They include:

The *trigeminal nerve*, which controls the muscles of chewing and facial expression, is also thought to be responsible for migraine headaches that can produce symptoms of extreme pain, dizziness, visual disturbances, and nausea.

The *intercostal nerves* that supply motor and sensory impulses to the thorax and abdomen are visible between each of the specimen's ribs.

The *phrenic nerve,* running through the center of the chest cavity and attaching to the diaphragm, causes the diaphragm to contract with each breath.

The *vagus nerve*, visible just to the left of the spinal column, controls much of our autonomic nervous system, including taste, digestion, and excretion. Because it is the longest of the cranial nerves—extending from the base of the brain to the solar plexus—the vagus nerve derives its name from the Latin word meaning "to wander." Under great stress or anxiety, this nerve may affect heart rate and slow the movement of food through the digestive tract.

facial nerve "duck's foot"

trigeminal nerve

intercostal nerve

vagus nerve

phrenic nerve

solar plexus

radial nerve

femoral nerve

median nerve

The opened cranial cavity at the back of this specimen exposes the brain's protective layers of bone and connective tissue called the cranial meninges. There are three layers of meninges: the dura mater, the arachnoid mater, and the innermost pia mater. The cranial meninges connect to the similarly protective spinal meninges through the foramen magnum opening at the base of the skull. Also visible are the dural sinuses, where de-oxygenated blood from the brain gathers before returning to the heart via the jugular vein.

The thickest and longest nerve in the body, the sciatic nerve, is also visible. Beginning in the buttocks, this nerve and its branches innervate, or supply nerve impulses to, the skin and muscles of the thigh, leg, and foot. Increased pressure on the sciatic nerve causes sciatica, a form of nerve damage characterized by sharp pains in the buttocks and leg. A common cause of sciatica is pressure from a herniated vertebral disc.

The nerves of the hand as they emerge from the carpal tunnel are visible on the specimen's left wrist (opposite page). The carpal tunnel is the site of the ailment known as carpal tunnel syndrome, a common malady today with our repetitive use of computers. The syndrome, characterized by numbness and pain in the thumb and middle fingers, occurs when tendons become inflamed and press on the median nerve where it passes through the carpal tunnel to the hand.

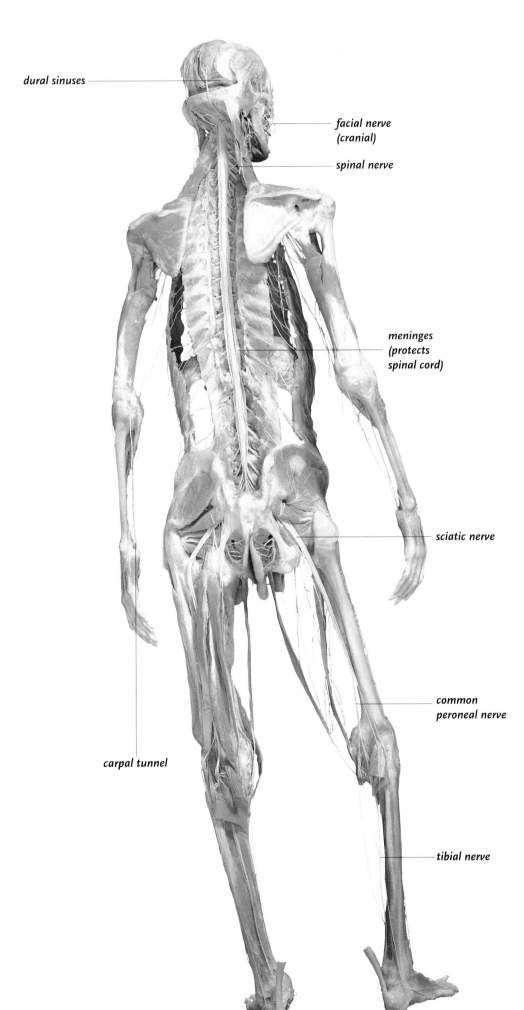

dural sinuses

facial nerve (cranial)

spinal nerve

meninges (protects spinal cord)

sciatic nerve

common peroneal nerve

carpal tunnel

tibial nerve

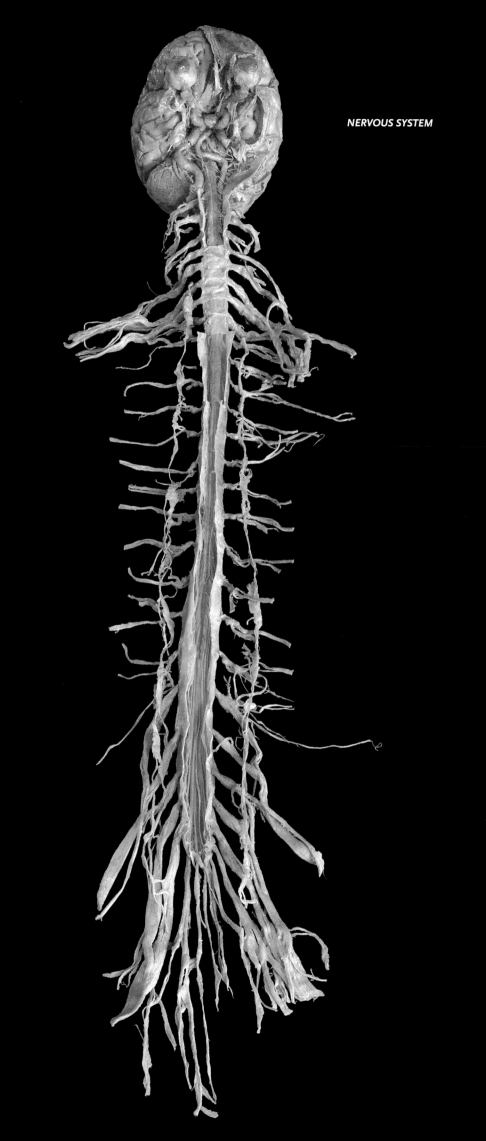

The brain is the mysterious organ of the nervous system and is essential for all bodily functions. It contains billions of nerve cells that are in constant communication with each other and with all parts of the body. These split-second communications most commonly take place when a nerve cell releases chemicals, which then interact with another nerve cell across a microscopic gap called a synapse.

The largest sections of the brain are the two cerebral hemispheres. Each half is covered with a layer of gray matter, the cerebral cortex. If spread out, the gray matter would cover more than three square feet. Gray matter serves as the seat of all higher brain functions, including consciousness, memory, thought, behavior, and personality.

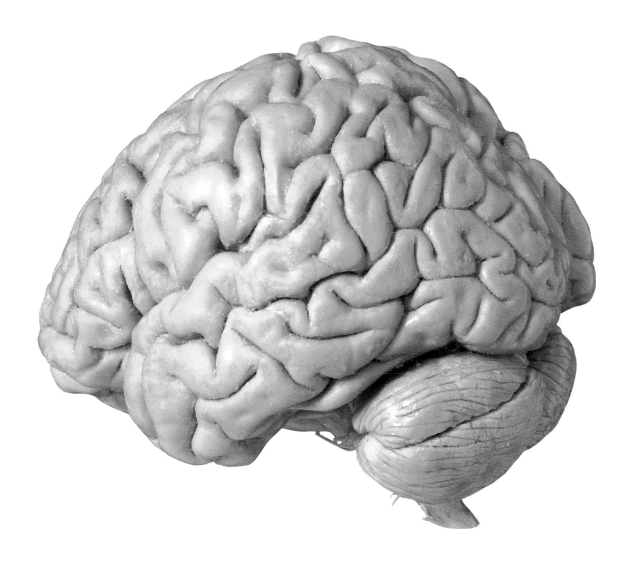

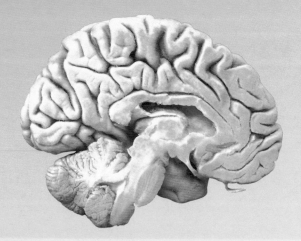

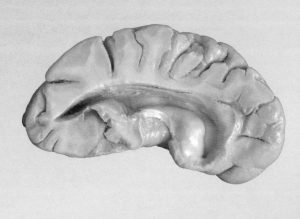

GYRUS AND CEREBRAL CORTEX (GRAY MATTER)

Due to its rapid growth through evolution, the cerebral hemispheres, which account for 40 percent of total brain mass, developed a series of folds that allow them to fit inside the skull. These folds give the surface, or gray matter, of the brain its wrinkled appearance and expand the brain's surface area several hundred times over. Each fold is called a gyrus and each of us has our own individual pattern.

The cerebral cortex is comprised of neurons (brain cells) that allow each hemisphere to perform its own series of unique functions. The left hemisphere of the brain is more dominant in speech, writing, and language skills; the right hemisphere in pictures and ideas.

Beneath the gray matter is the white matter made up of nerve fibers that transmit information, such as muscle movement and speech, into and out of the cerebral cortex.

HIPPOCAMPUS

This deep fold in the central part of the cerebral hemisphere is named after its resemblance to a sea horse (*hippos kampos*—Greek for "horse sea monster"). The hippocampus is an important part of a larger group of structures that make up the limbic system, which helps regulate the mechanisms underlying emotion and behavior. It is also an essential site for the formation of short-term memory and one of the regions first affected by Alzheimer's disease.

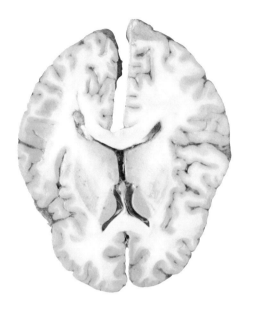

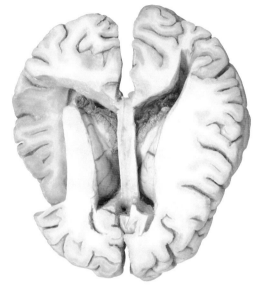

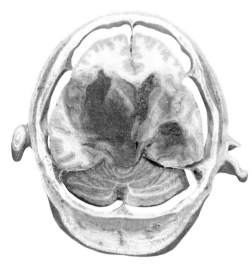

BRAIN VENTRICLES AND CEREBROSPINAL FLUID

Inside the brain are an interconnected series of hollow spaces called ventricles. They are filled with a clear water-like fluid called cerebrospinal fluid (CSF). Made within the ventricles, this fluid circulates between layers of the meninges, the protective membranes that surround the brain. It also circulates in the meninges surrounding the spinal cord. CSF provides buoyancy for the brain and cushions it from blows against the skull. In addition, it helps move wastes produced by the brain and spinal cord into the bloodstream to be eliminated from the body through the lungs and the kidneys

The cerebrospinal fluid is continuously produced, circulated, and reabsorbed once every six hours. If a blockage prevents the cerebrospinal fluid from circulating, the ventricles can enlarge, putting pressure on the brain. This condition is known as hydrocephalus (water on the brain).

STROKE

The brain requires a massive and continual blood supply. If this blood supply is interrupted for even a few moments, brain tissues will begin to die.

This is the case with stroke, which is caused by a blockage (thrombosis) or rupture in one or more of the brain's blood vessels. A broken vessel fills a portion of the brain, increasing pressure, and leading to further tissue death. Those with high blood pressure and arteriosclerosis are at a greater risk for stroke, which can produce paralysis, as well as language and vision impairment.

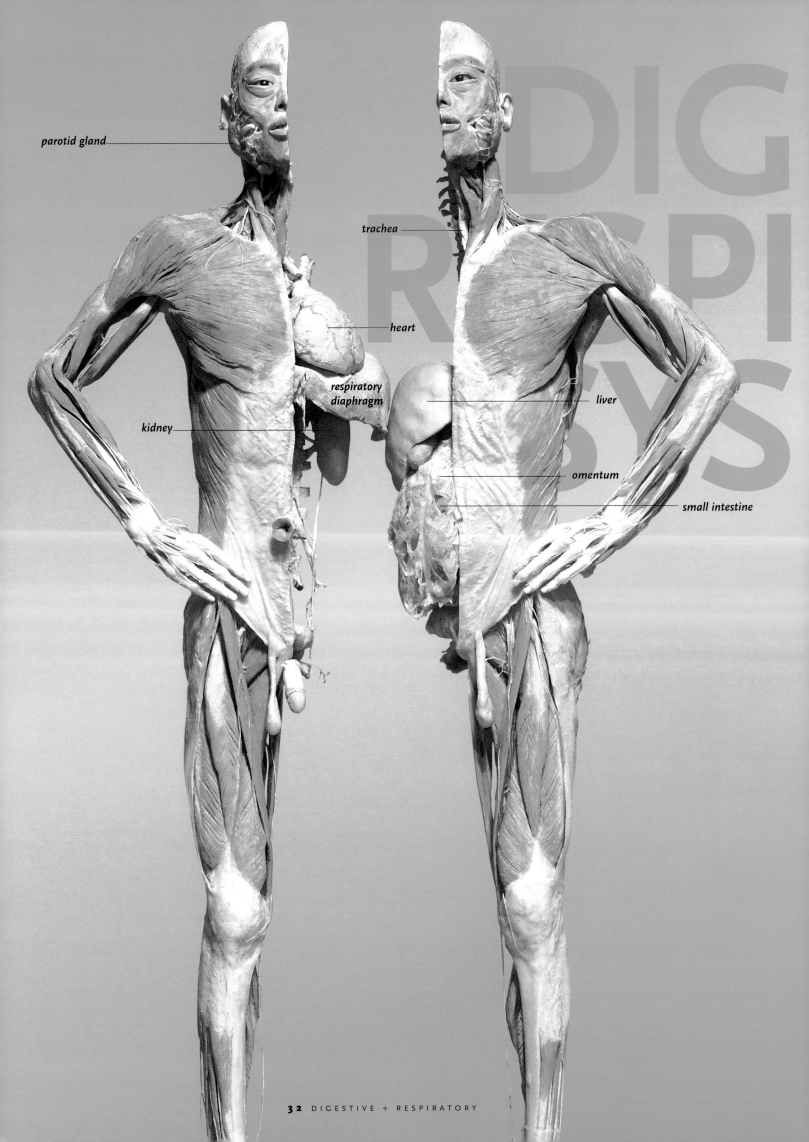

parotid gland

trachea

heart

respiratory
diaphragm

kidney

liver

omentum

small intestine

ESTIVE + RATORY TEM

aorta

intervertebral discs

vertebra

colon

This sagittal dissection provides a rare view into the compact and complex relationships that exist between the body's major organs. As can be clearly seen, the main organs that occupy the thorax, or chest cavity, are the lungs and heart. It is here that the oxygen is extracted from the outside air and circulated into the bloodstream where it is transported to every cell in the body. The heart's placement between the lungs makes clear its central role in respiration and circulation. The abdominal cavity, separated from the thoracic cavity by the muscular respiratory diaphragm, contains several important digestive organs: the stomach, small and large intestines, liver, and pancreas.

More than twenty feet in length, our digestive tracts fit within the relatively small confines of the abdominal cavity. No space is wasted: the liver and pancreas fit neatly around the stomach and the first part of the small intestine (the duodenum); the gallbladder tucks behind the liver. The coils of the small intestine and large intestine are covered by the greater omentum, an apron of tissue that attaches to and covers the stomach. A connective tissue, the omentum, carries nerves and blood vessels to and from the digestive organs and guards them against infection. In an overweight person, the omentum also contains large quantities of fat, which produce a "pot belly" with loss of muscle tone.

In this specimen, the thoracic and abdominal cavities have been exposed to reveal the position of the main organs within these areas.

THORACIC CAVITY

In the thoracic cavity, the tissue of the right lung has been removed, exposing the bronchial tree and an enlarged heart enclosed in its protective sac called the pericardium. An enlargerd heart often results from lack of oxygen to the heart muscle or high blood pressure. These factors make the heart work harder causing it to grow in compensation. An enlarged heart does not necessarily mean a stronger heart. If the strains on a heart are not reduced, the risk of heart attack increases dramatically.

ABDOMINAL CAVITY

A look into the dissected abdomen reveals the close relationship between the duodenum, liver, and the pancreas. The liver and pancreas secrete the enzymes essential to digestion through a series of ducts leading into the duodenum, the first ten inches of the small intestine. Within the duodenum, ingested food is broken down into nutrients the body can use for fuel. These nutrients are not available to the body until they are absorbed through the intestine wall, enter the bloodstream, and are transported to the liver for further processing and storage.

The pancreas also produces insulin, which helps regulate the level of glucose in our blood. Glucose, a type of sugar, is the main energy source for our cells. Any excess glucose is stored in the liver until needed by the body. When pancreatic cells cannot produce enough insulin and glucose levels in the body rise, the disease diabetes mellitus occurs.

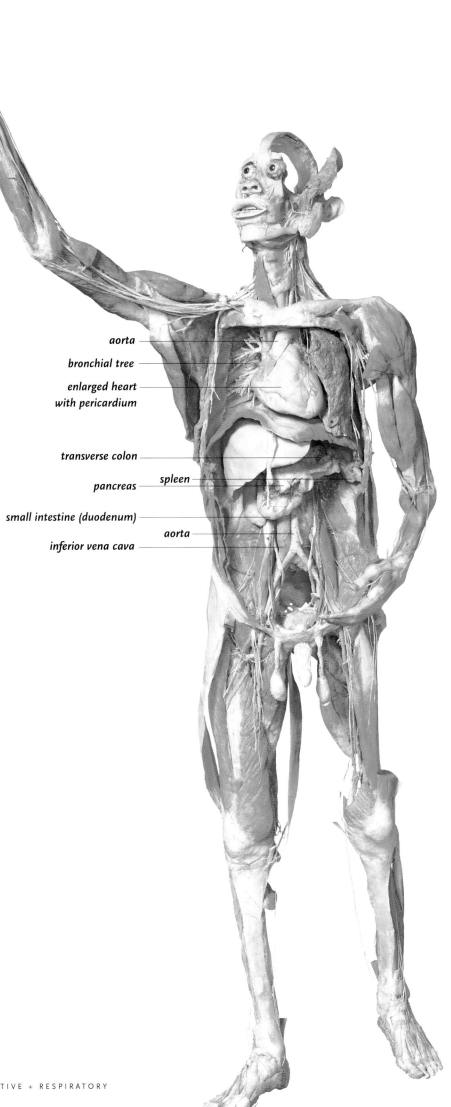

aorta

bronchial tree

enlarged heart with pericardium

transverse colon

pancreas — spleen

small intestine (duodenum)

aorta

inferior vena cava

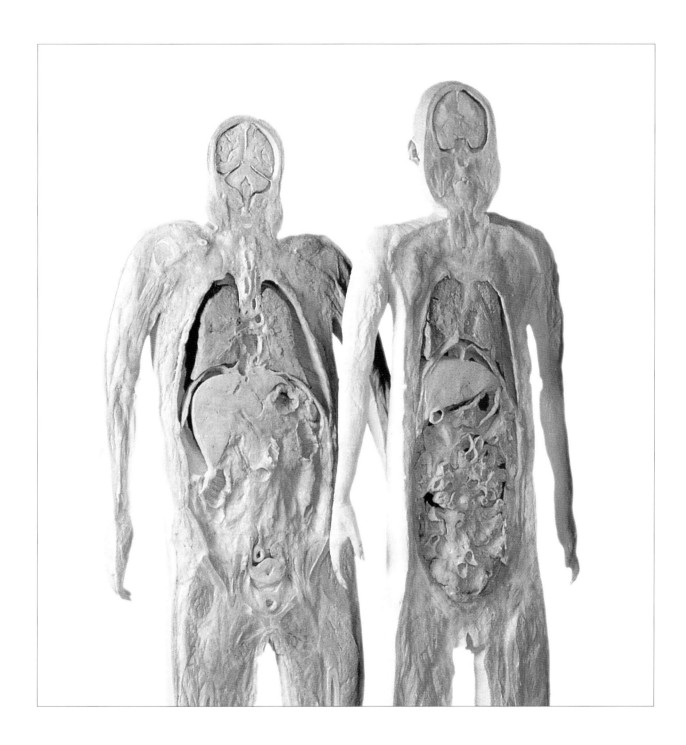

ADIPOSE (FAT) TISSUE

Adipose tissue protects and supports the organs, acts as an insulator, and serves as an important energy reserve in case of need. Excessive fat build-up in the connective tissues can lead to a greater risk for heart attack, stroke, diabetes, arthritis, and cancer. This build-up, obesity, is caused by numerous factors: illness, medication, genetics, stress, and overeating. It is on the rise in industrialized nations.

TONGUE, PHARYNX, TRACHEA, AND ESOPHAGUS

Digestion of food begins in the mouth, with the teeth, and tongue. The teeth tear, bite, and grind food, mixing it with saliva. The muscular tongue moves food between the teeth to assist in chewing and swallowing. When food is swallowed, a cartilaginous flap of tissue, called the epiglottis, closes off the airway to prevent us from choking. Food then enters the esophagus, a ten-inch-long muscular tube, where it is transported to the stomach by peristalsis (muscular contractions), which occurs throughout the digestive tract.

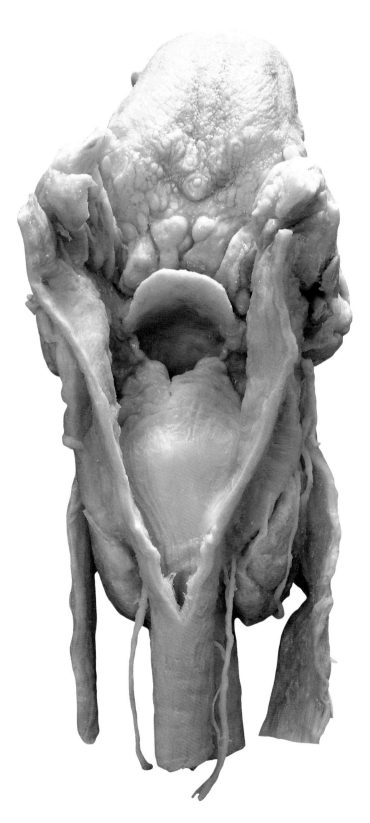

TASTE

Taste buds lie in the grooves between the bumps (papillae) on your tongue. They contain chemical receptors for specific tastes, which are replaced every ten days. The taste buds at the tip of the tongue are most sensitive to sweet, while the sides of the tongue are most sensitive to salty and sour tastes. The chemical receptors at the back of the tongue react to the bitter in our diets.

When the tiny fibers within our taste buds bind with molecules of food, they send impulses to the brain. The brain uses this information to determine the nature of the food we are eating and releases digestive enzymes needed to break down that food.

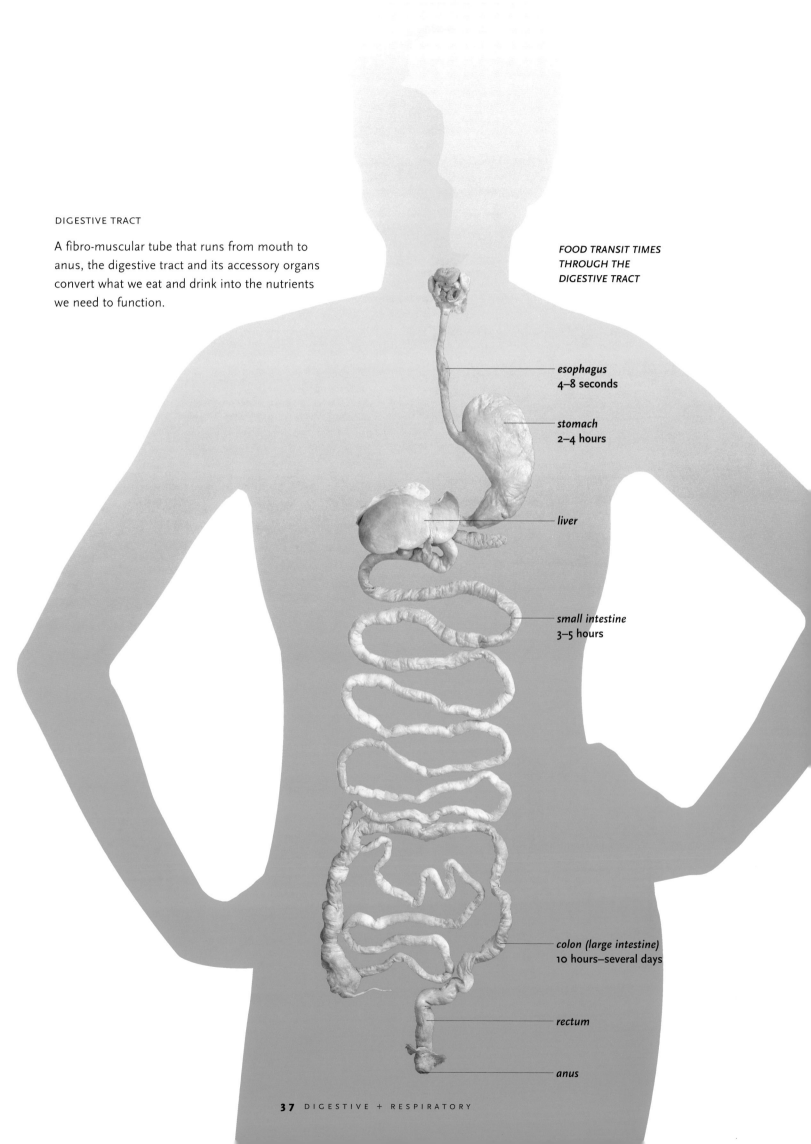

DIGESTIVE TRACT

A fibro-muscular tube that runs from mouth to anus, the digestive tract and its accessory organs convert what we eat and drink into the nutrients we need to function.

FOOD TRANSIT TIMES THROUGH THE DIGESTIVE TRACT

esophagus
4–8 seconds

stomach
2–4 hours

liver

small intestine
3–5 hours

colon (large intestine)
10 hours–several days

rectum

anus

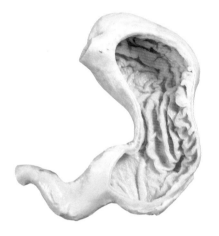
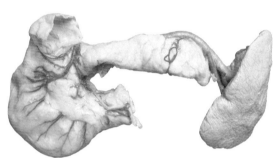

STOMACH WITH RUGAE

In the stomach, three layers of muscle churn partially digested food with powerful gastric juices, turning the food into a paste-like substance and killing many bacteria that might otherwise bring disease to the body.

The stomach contains many nonpermanent internal folds called rugae. These folds are present when the stomach is empty, but stretch out when we eat, creating more space for food. Cells within the rugae produce mucus, enzymes, and strong hydrochloric acid. The enzymes and acid break down food, while the mucus protects the stomach from being digested. We feel full when nerve receptors in the stomach tell the brain that the stomach has stretched enough.

DUODENUM WITH PANCREAS AND SPLEEN

The duodenum, visible on the left of the specimen above, is a ten-inch, C-shaped segment at the beginning of the small intestine. As the stomach releases food into it, the duodenum secretes mucus and bicarbonate to neutralize stomach acids.

The pancreas, center, then secretes juices into the duodenum to digest carbohydrates, proteins, nucleic acids, and fats—the four types of nutrients the body needs for life. Bile, produced by the liver and stored in the gallbladder, also enters the duodenum at this time to aid in the breakdown of fats.

The spleen, on the right of the specimen, helps form blood in the developing fetus and, though not essential to an adult, continues to filter blood and fight disease throughout life.

SECTION OF SMALL INTESTINE

The small intestine performs most of the digestion and absorption of nutrients in the digestive tract. More than ten feet long, the small intestine contains several million villi and microvilli. These microscopic, fingerlike projections reach into the hollow spaces of the intestine and increase the small intestine's surface area a thousand times. Digested molecules pass through these projections into the bloodstream where they are carried to the liver for further processing.

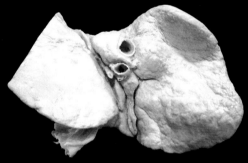

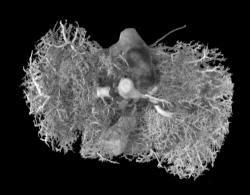

LIVER

The second heaviest organ of the body (after the skin) and weighing close to 3.5 pounds in an average adult, the liver performs many important functions. It produces bile, key to the proper digestion of fats. It also stores vitamin A and produces several proteins essential to normal blood flow and clotting. In addition, the liver is one of the body's main storage centers for fats, amino acids, and, most importantly, glucose, which it extracts from blood returning from the digestive tract.

CIRRHOTIC LIVER

The liver also plays an important role in removing and destroying waste products and ingested toxins from the blood, including alcohol, drugs, and microbes. Improper diet, which often accompanies alcohol and drug abuse, can lead to the death of liver cells and their replacement by scar tissue. This disease is known as cirrhosis and is visible on the above specimen. Other diseases, such as liver cancer and hepatitis (inflammation of the liver), can also severely damage the liver. A liver transplant is often the only way to treat these serious life-threatening conditions.

LIVER BLOOD SUPPLY AND GALLBLADDER

This special dissection reveals the inner architecture of the liver, in particular the pathway that blood takes through the organ. Two types of blood enter the liver: oxygen-rich blood from the heart and nutrient-rich blood from the intestines. As blood from both sources mixes and passes toward the center of the liver, nutrients are extracted from it, the liver cells are nourished, and the blood is cleansed and fortified. Bile, essential for the proper digestion of fats, flows via separate ducts in the reverse direction, from the center of the liver toward its surface. Here it leaves the liver and is stored in the gallbladder (green pouch) until it is needed for digestion.

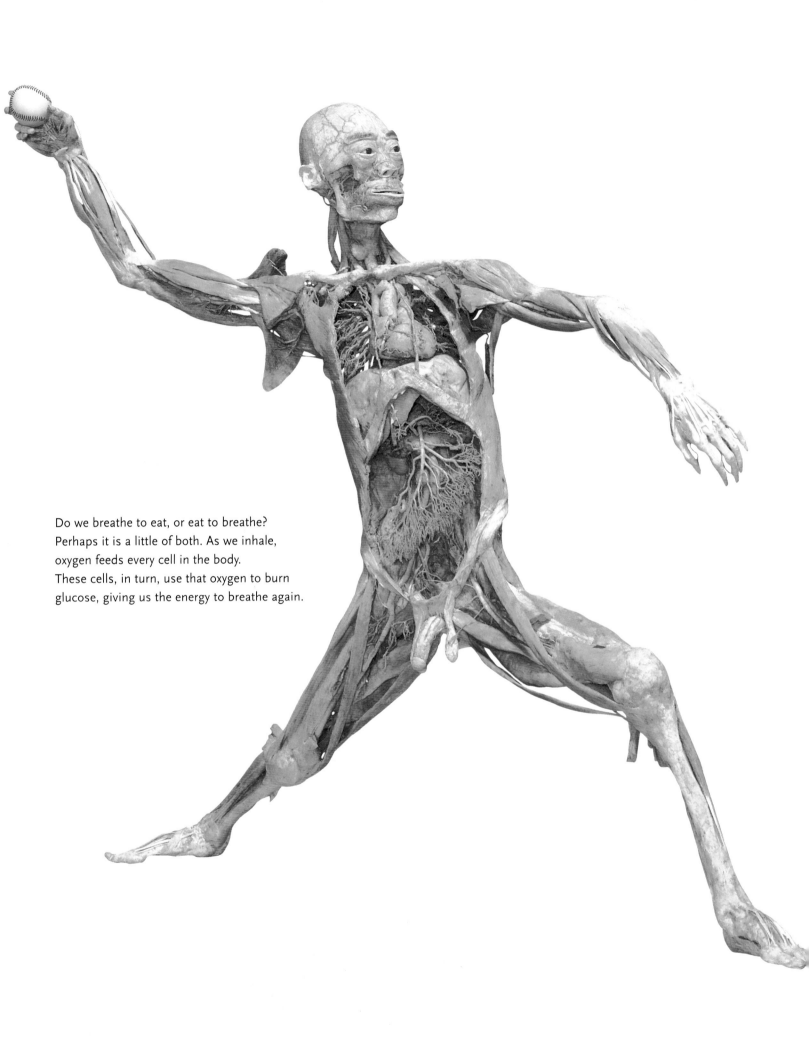

Do we breathe to eat, or eat to breathe?
Perhaps it is a little of both. As we inhale,
oxygen feeds every cell in the body.
These cells, in turn, use that oxygen to burn
glucose, giving us the energy to breathe again.

"The heart is the king and the lungs are its ministers."

This statement made over four thousand years ago by Chinese physician Hwang Ti, is clearly evident with this specimen. While the lungs are responsible for inhaling oxygen into the blood stream, the heart must first circulate blood to the lungs to absorb that oxygen. The position of the heart between the lungs points to its central (and kingly) role in respiration and circulation.

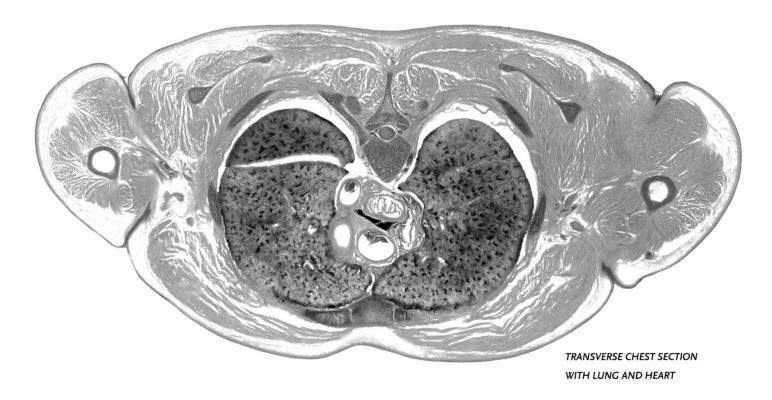

TRANSVERSE CHEST SECTION
WITH LUNG AND HEART

SEGMENTAL BRONCHI

As its name suggests, the bronchial tree branches into smaller and smaller segments as it enters the lungs. Despite its many branches, which eventually end at one of millions of alveoli where carbon dioxide is exchanged for oxygen, the bronchial tree is actually divided into only 20 segments. These segments are functionally separate regions in each lung. Each receives its own blood supply and can continue to operate if another segment is removed. This is nature's way of insuring that breathing will continue if other parts of the lung become diseased.

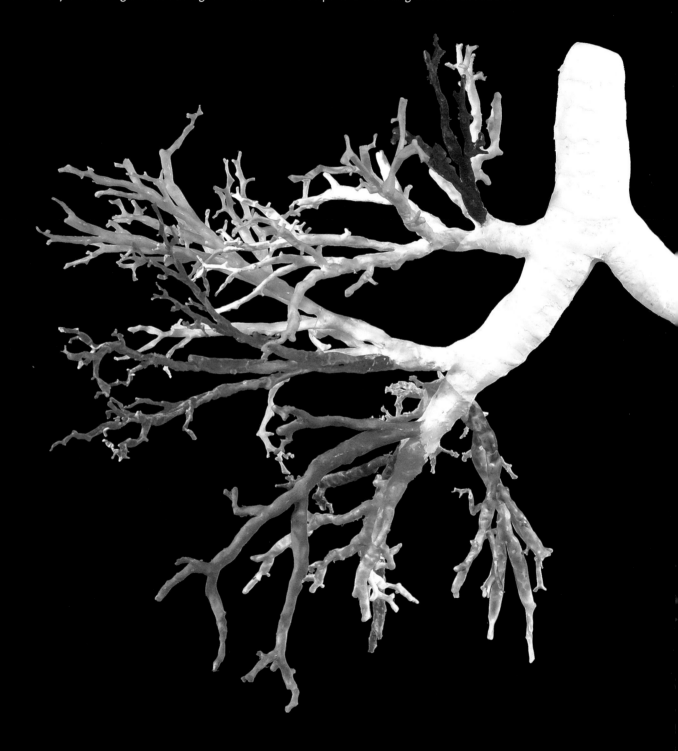

LARYNX, TRACHEA, AND BRONCHIAL TREE

This specimen displays structures of the upper airway, trachea, and lungs, which include:

Larynx Located in the front of the throat, it consists of the vocal cords and the epiglottis, which closes during swallowing to prevent choking.

Thyroid cartilage Also know as the "Adam's apple," it protects the front of the larynx and the vocal cords.

Trachea The pathway to the bronchial tree. Instead of fluid or muscle, which would block breathing, the trachea is kept open by 15 to 20 C-shaped cartilages.

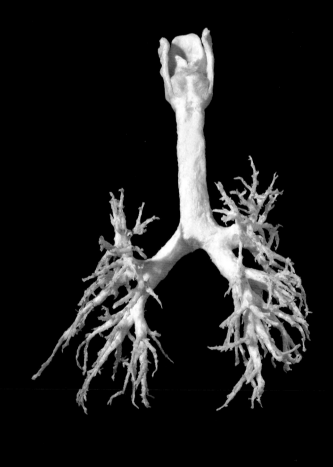

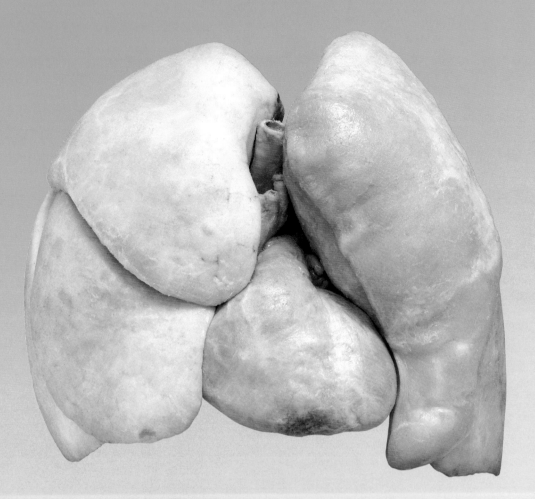

HEALTHY HEART AND LUNGS

A healthy pair of lungs contains more than three hundred million alveoli, the site where internal respiration occurs. If spread out, all these alveoli would cover a tennis court.

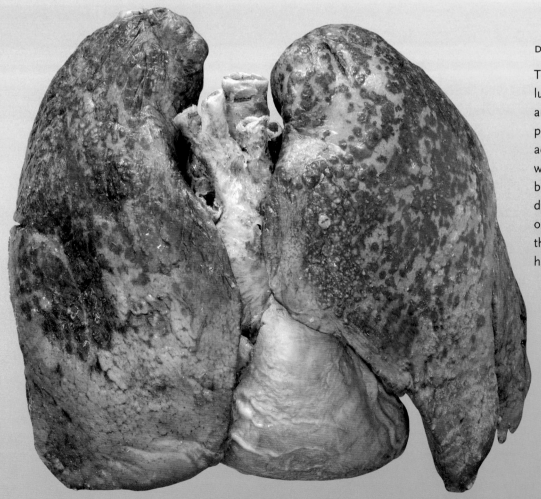

DISEASED LUNGS

These shrunken and darkened lungs illustrate the tar build-up and disease that often accompanies cigarette smoking. The accumulation of smoking debris within the lungs leads to the breakdown of the alveoli, greatly decreasing the surface area for oxygen exchange, which causes the rest of the organs to work harder with less oxygen.

HEALTHY HEART   *INSIDE THE HEART*

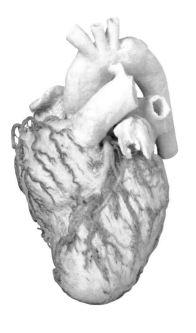
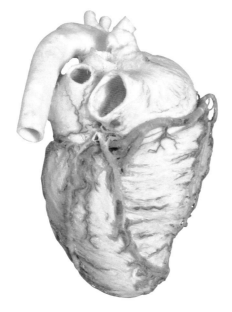
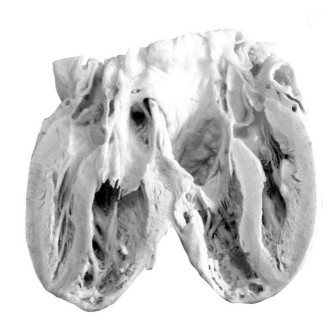

THAT TICKING SOUND

The heart is a two-chambered, never ceasing pump, which contracts 60 to 80 times per minute. The sound doctors hear when they put a stethoscope to your chest is not the sound of the heart moving, but the sound of its valves closing as they push 4,300 gallons of blood through the heart every day. (A heart murmur is an indication that the heart valves are not closing properly, thus allowing blood to leak around them.)

The heart is basically a pear-shaped, not a heart-shaped, shell with two chambers at the top called the atria and two at the bottom called the ventricles. Each atrium is connected by a valve to the ventricle below. As their name suggests, the atria are the chambers that receive the blood from the body or lungs as it enters the heart and which allow this blood to continue its flow into the ventricles. Once filled with blood, the cardiac muscles in the walls of the ventricles contract, forcing the blood out of the heart. The more muscular left ventricle pumps blood to the far reaches of the body; the right ventricle pumps blood a shorter distance to the lungs.

The continuous contraction (heartbeat) of the heart is necessary to maintain the life-giving flow of blood to every cell, tissue, and organ of your body. Each of these heartbeats originates in the sinoatrial node, which lies on the back wall of the right atrium. The sinoatrial node generates an electrical pulse, which causes the atria to contract simultaneously, and the ventricles to contract an instant later. Every heartbeat of your life is regulated in this way, without your having to do anything about it. If anything goes wrong with the node, an artificial pacemaker can be implanted to return your heart to its proper rhythm.

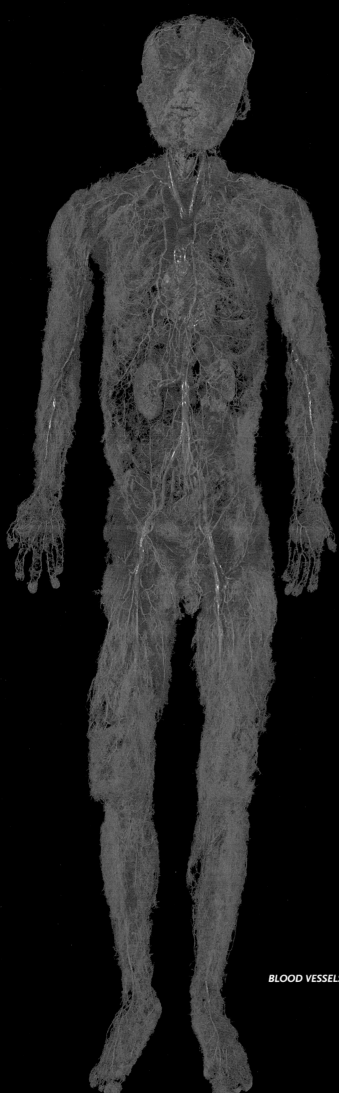

The circulatory system is the body's superhighway. This closed ring, composed of the heart and its attached blood vessels (arteries and veins), transports everything our cells need to support their normal function, most importantly oxygen, absorbed nutrients, and a variety of hormones. No cell of the body lies more than a few micrometers from one of the body's 60,000 miles of blood vessels. It takes less than 60 seconds for a drop of blood to transit this complicated and delicate life-giving system.

CIRC
SYST

BLOOD VESSELS OF THE BODY

ULATORY
EM

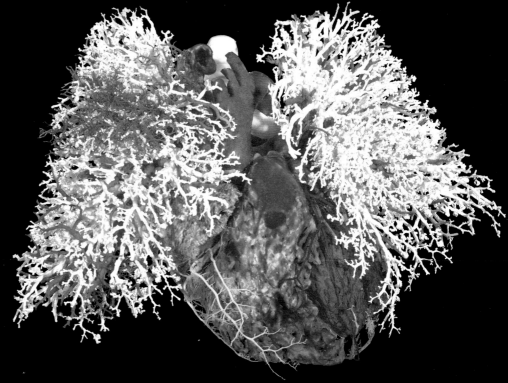

BRONCHIAL TREE, PULMONARY VEINS, AND HEART

The specimens on these and the following pages were prepared using a special casting method. The blood vessels were first injected with a colored polymer. Once the polymer hardened, the remaining body tissue was removed by a corrosive chemical to reveal the blood vessels' intricate matrix.

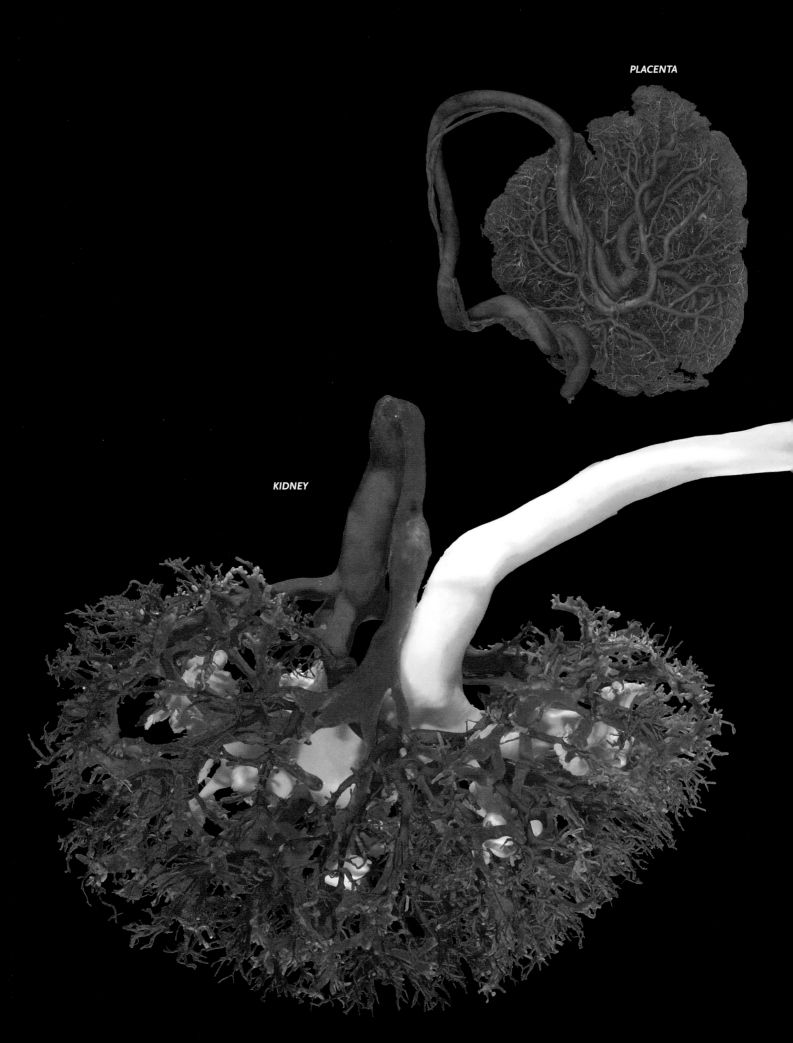

PLACENTA

KIDNEY

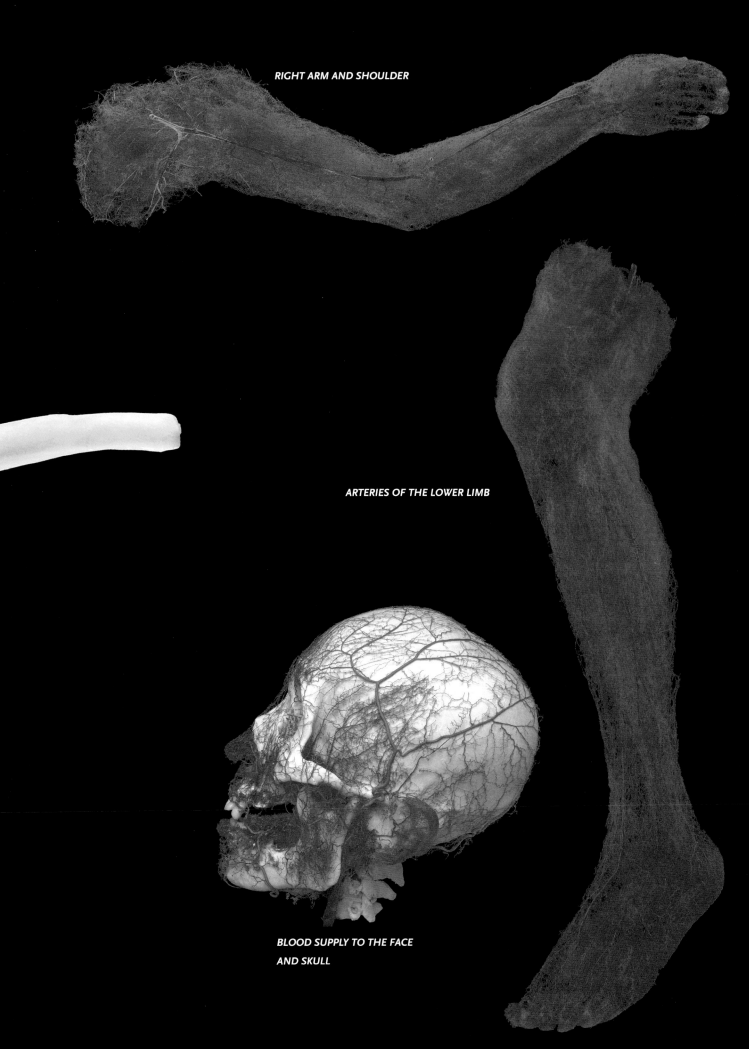

RIGHT ARM AND SHOULDER

ARTERIES OF THE LOWER LIMB

BLOOD SUPPLY TO THE FACE
AND SKULL

REPROD URINARY SYSTEM

Although closely associated, the reproductive and urinary systems serve different purposes. The urinary system collects metabolic waste products from the blood and removes them from the body, maintaining the proper balance of water and electrolytes in the body.

The reproductive system's purpose is to see to the continuation of the species. Chromosomes are the small threads in every cell that store your individual genetic code, the pattern of your life, your heredity. There are 46 chromosomes in each of our cells, but the female sex cell, the egg, and the male sex cell, the sperm have only 23. Only when the egg and sperm combine is a new cell created that is capable of developing into a human.

The whole body specimen at right illustrates features of the female reproductive system, including: mammary glands, uterus, uterine (Fallopian) tubes, and the external genitalia.

THE BREASTS

The breasts, or mammary glands, consist of glandular tissue embedded in fat. These tissues are held in place by ligaments that attach to the deep layer of the skin. The breasts are the source of milk produced in large amounts following the birth of a baby. A series of ducts carry milk from the glands to the nipples where it is expelled during nursing through the contraction of smooth muscle and the infant's suckling.

Breast cancer is the most common cancer for women in industrial nations and, along with lung cancer, is one of the leading causes of cancer death in women. The cancer begins in the milk ducts of the breast and first manifests as a hard, immovable lump. While its cause is unclear, excess estrogen and genetic factors seem to contribute to its onset. Early detection is crucial to surviving breast cancer; as the cancer grows, it can spread to the lymphatic system, bloodstream, lungs, and even attack the skin.

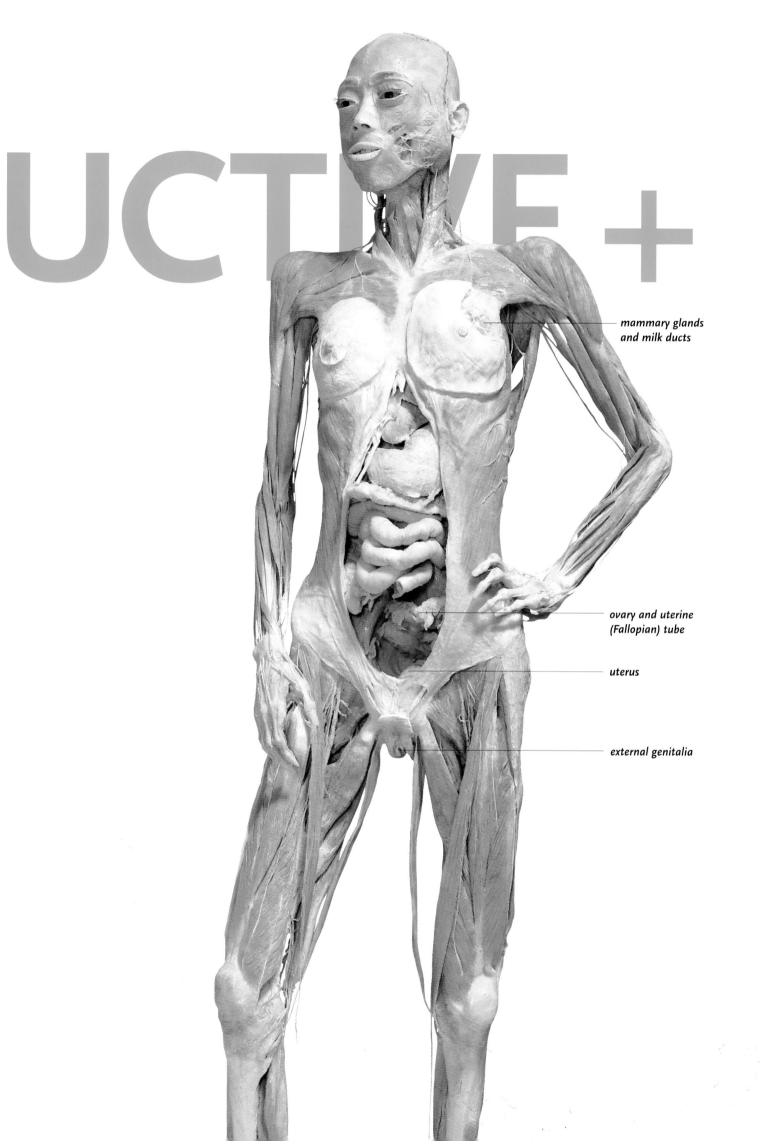

mammary glands
and milk ducts

ovary and uterine
(Fallopian) tube

uterus

external genitalia

UCTIVE +

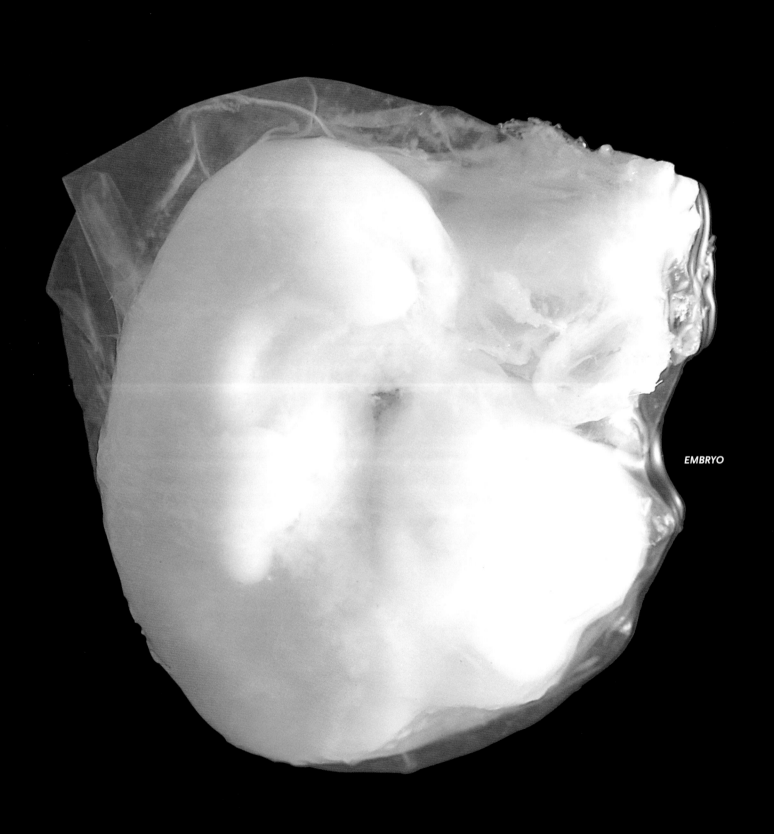

EMBRYO

The 40 weeks of *in utero* development are divided into two extended time periods: the embryonic period that runs through the end of the eighth week of gestation; and the fetal period, which extends from the ninth week until birth. The embryonic period is characterized by the development of all the major organ systems, while the fetal period is characterized primarily by their increased growth.

PLACENTA

The placenta is a temporary organ that forms within the wall of the uterus after conception from a combination of uterine and fetal tissue. There is no mixing of embryonic and maternal blood in the placenta. Instead, all exchange between these two separate circulations takes place across a very thin cellular barrier, which protects the developing fetus against harmful substances. However, the placental barrier cannot stop harmful chemicals, alcohol or viruses. If such substances are ingested during the embryonic period, they can cause birth defects and have other serious consequences on the process of normal development.

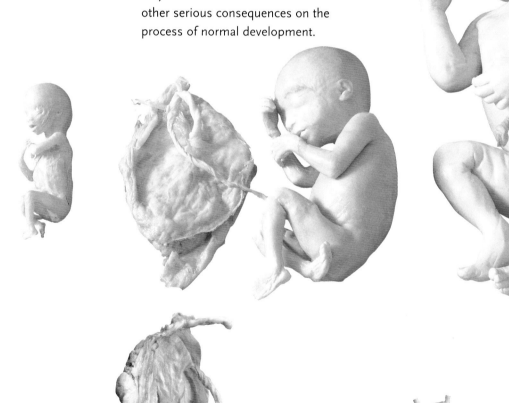

PLACENTA OF TWINS

INFANT HEART AND LUNGS

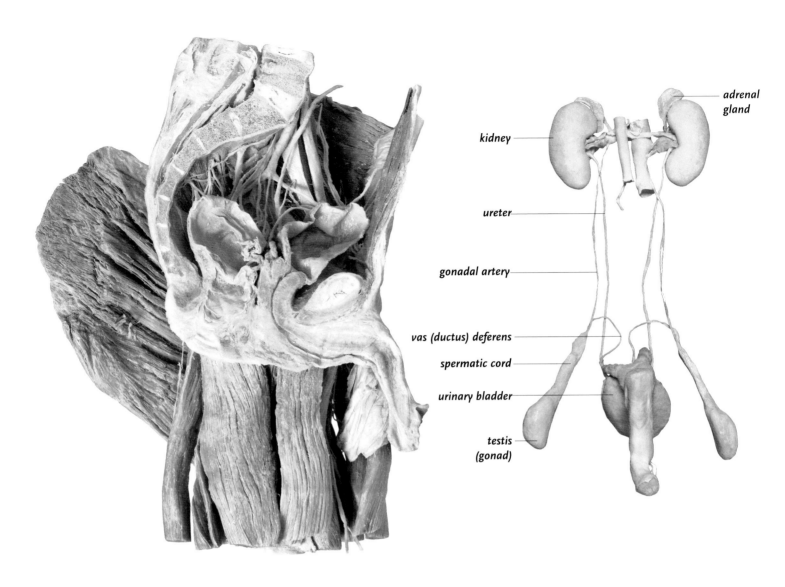

kidney

adrenal gland

ureter

gonadal artery

vas (ductus) deferens

spermatic cord

urinary bladder

testis (gonad)

CROSS SECTION OF PENIS

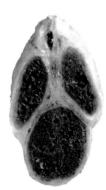

THE URINARY SYSTEM: KIDNEYS, URETERS, AND BLADDER

The kidneys filter almost three pints of blood per minute, removing waste products and creating urine in the process. Urine travels by muscular contractions through the ureters, one drop at a time, to the bladder where it is stored. Our bladders can hold approximately 1.5 pints. Pressure receptors in the bladder alert the brain as the bladder fills. If the bladder reaches two-thirds capacity, the urge to empty it is conveyed to the brain.

MALE REPRODUCTIVE SYSTEM

The male reproductive system includes: the penis, the testes that produce sperm and male hormones, plus several ducts and glands that transport sperm and create semen.

Testes The testes are two oval organs contained in the scrotum that create sperm, the male sex cell essential to reproduction. The testes best produce sperm at two degrees below normal body temperature. For this reason, they are contained within the scrotum, but outside the body cavity.

Penis The penis contains three cylinders of spongy erectile tissue, which fill with blood when the male becomes aroused. The urethra passes through the penis, transporting urine and seminal fluids out of the body.

Spermatic cord The spermatic cord contains the spermatic artery, which supplies the testes with blood, and the vas deferens, which transports sperm from the testes to the prostate gland and seminal vesicles adding nutrients and fluid to the sperm as it travels out of the body as semen.

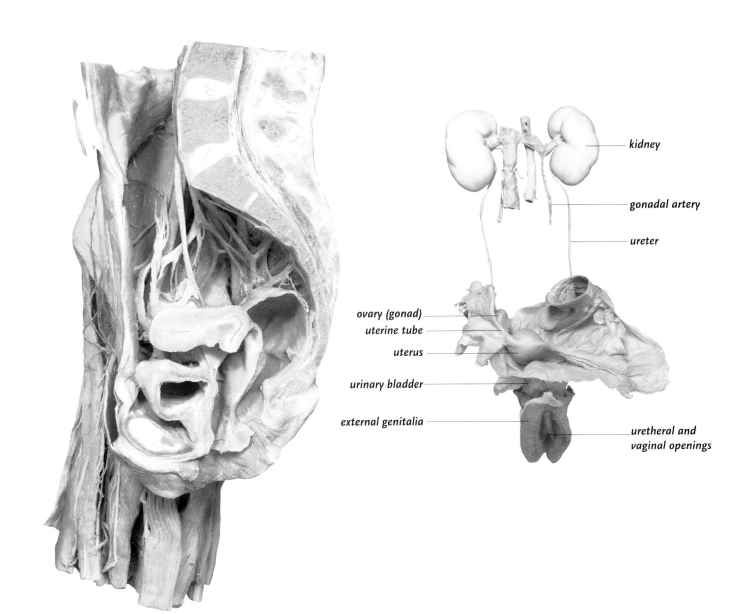

kidney

gonadal artery

ureter

ovary (gonad)

uterine tube

uterus

urinary bladder

external genitalia

uretheral and
vaginal openings

FEMALE REPRODUCTIVE SYSTEM

Located in the pelvic cavity behind the juncture of the hipbones, the female reproductive organs include:

Ovaries   These small oval-shaped organs lie close to the uterine tubes. They are the source of the female sex cells called ova (eggs) and the female reproductive hormones that assist in the development of the female reproductive system and play an important role in the reproductive cycle.

Uterine (Fallopian) Tubes   These paired, narrow tubes receive the egg cells released from the ovaries (ovulation) and transport them to the uterus. It is within these tubes that fertilization (union of an egg and sperm cell) normally occurs.

Uterus   Also called the "womb," the wall of this muscular organ provides the site where embryonic and fetal development occurs. Located above the urinary bladder, the uterus can expand during pregnancy to more than 20 times in size, often placing pressure on the bladder.

**KIDNEY WITH
CORONAL CUT**

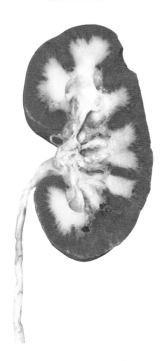

isease is a part of life, so is our desire to overcome it. Guided by the continued study of human anatomy and the availability of specimens such as those in the Exhibition, physicians and medical researchers are developing new techniques, instruments, and medications to address the most pressing health issues of our day. This deeper understanding of the body is allowing us to live longer, healthier lives.

THE TREATE

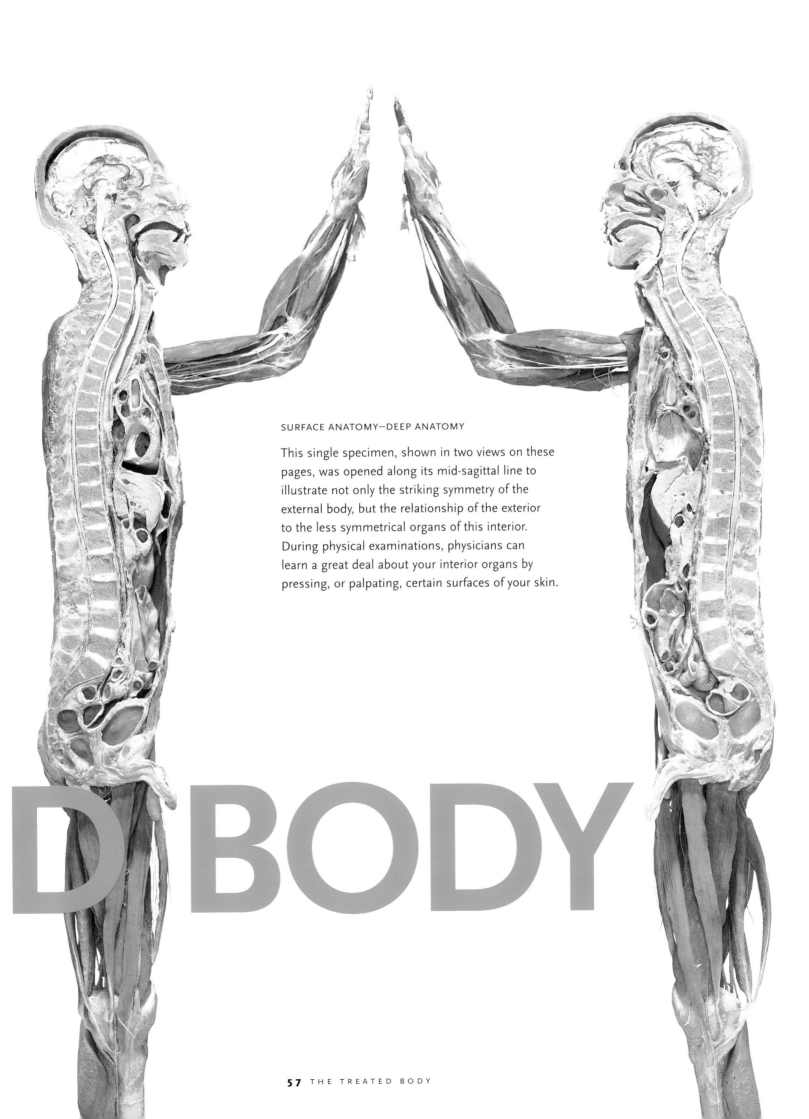

SURFACE ANATOMY—DEEP ANATOMY

This single specimen, shown in two views on these pages, was opened along its mid-sagittal line to illustrate not only the striking symmetry of the external body, but the relationship of the exterior to the less symmetrical organs of this interior. During physical examinations, physicians can learn a great deal about your interior organs by pressing, or palpating, certain surfaces of your skin.

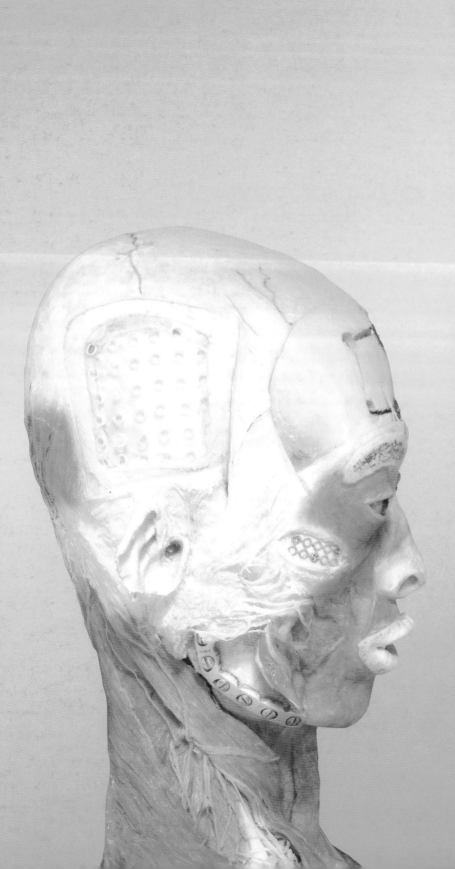

MEDICAL PROSTHESES AND SURGICAL TOOLS

The specimen on this and the adjacent page illustrates techniques used to heal or replace damaged bones, as well as the surgical tools that assist in these orthopedic procedures and others such as closure after brain surgery.

Bone has an amazing ability to mend itself when broken. Optimal healing occurs when the broken ends of the bone are properly aligned. For this reason, surgeons often use plates and screws to stabilize broken bones, keeping them fixed in place as they heal. Metal shafts, similar to that in the thigh of the specimen, provide a template around which shattered bones can reconnect. Surgeons access these areas by use of muscle spreaders of various sizes and configurations depending on application.

Due to disease or a lifetime of use, the joint surfaces of bones may deteriorate, causing debilitating pain. In these cases, a prosthesis or artificial replacement joint is needed. Made often of stainless steel or titanium, the new joint is cemented into the bone, taking the place of the defective one.

Attempting to lengthen the life of an effective joint implant, researchers are now making new prosthetic surfaces from ceramics in an effort to prevent even the smallest amount of corrosion. Many implants have a honeycomb as part of their design. This arrangement of open spaces is coated with bone cells to help the artificial joint bond more securely to the existing bone.

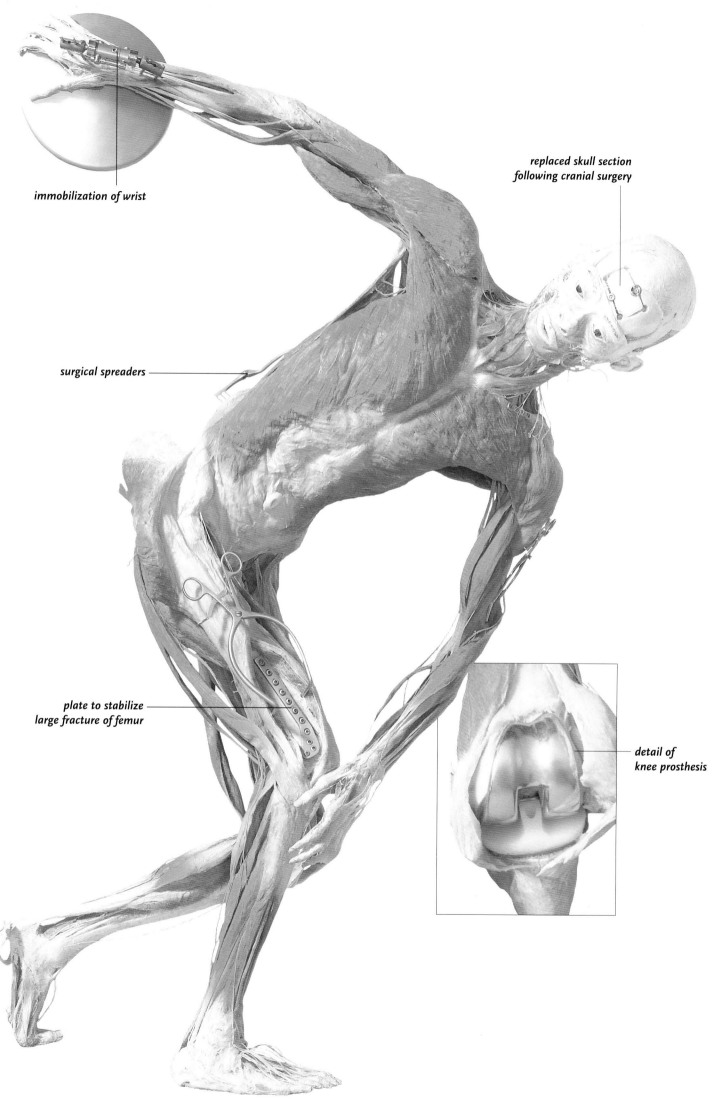

immobilization of wrist

replaced skull section
following cranial surgery

surgical spreaders

plate to stabilize
large fracture of femur

detail of
knee prosthesis

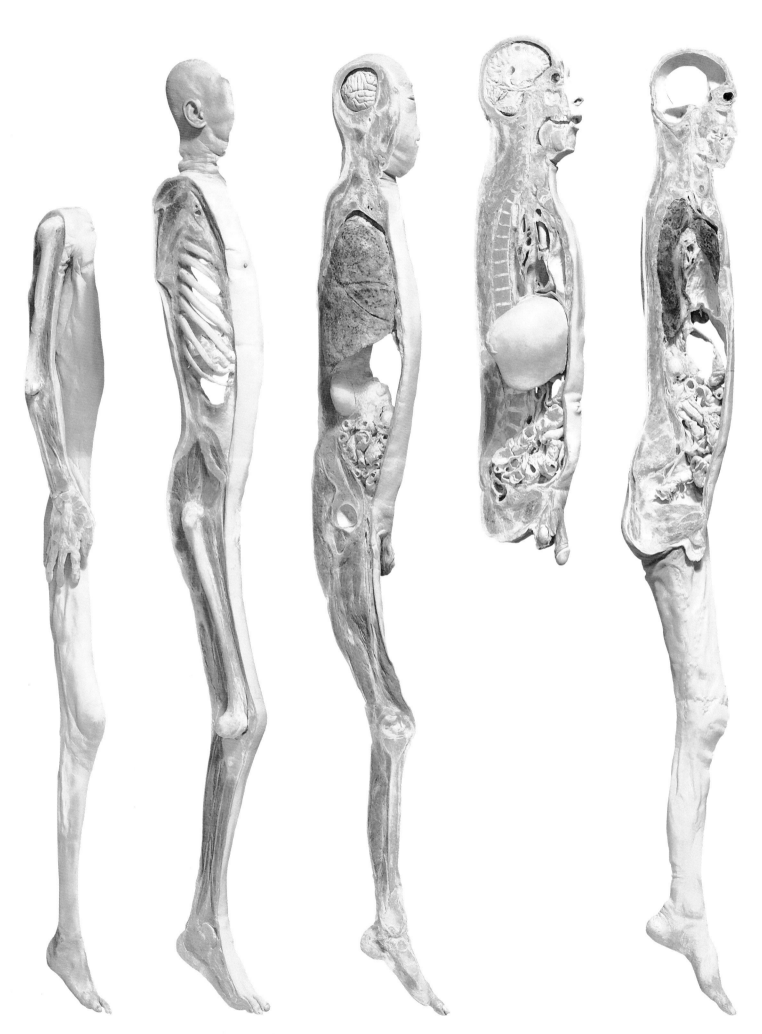

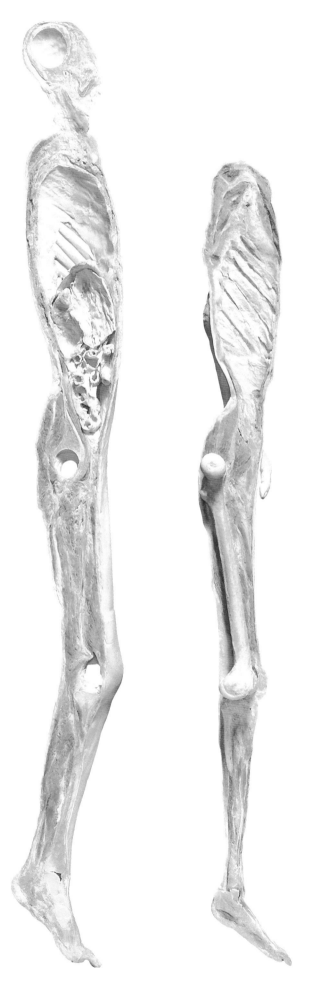

These thick sagittal sections show you in actuality one way that advanced diagnostic equipment, such as magnetic resonance instruments (MRI), "see" the body. MRI use powerful electromagnets to stimulate hydrogen atoms in the body. These moving atoms create radio signals, which are converted into detailed images that physicians can use to diagnose and pinpoint disease, making surgery and treatment more accurate and efficient.

But for all of its magic, MRI is a relatively old technique. Today, medical science is not only surrounding the body with machinery but taking it into the body itself. Small cameras can travel through the digestive tract examining every square millimeter of tissue, and robots are now used to assist in precise surgical techniques, sometimes controlled by surgeons from a remote location. Medicine is moving beyond circuitry and into the chemistry of the body itself. The entire human genome has been mapped and is being decoded; soon pharmaceuticals will be tailored to your specific genetic code. Stem cell research is helping us understand how the body develops and heals itself, changing the way we think about curing disease. And yet many challenges remain...

Yes, we live in a world surrounded by technology, information, and cement; fast-paced living with no time for reflection. We become ill and expect a physician to heal us swiftly, so we can return to our hectic way of life.

When an illness is severe and our mortality comes into question, we may take the time to stop and ponder our existence. But cured, we are off again, not thinking about the extraordinary, complicated human beings that we are.

Our bodies are indeed intricately more complex and wondrous than all of the computers and gadgetry that surround us today. Yet many of us do not really know what lies beneath our skin—how our bodies function, what they need to survive, what destroys them, what revives them.

BODIES...THE EXHIBITION is an attempt to remedy this unfortunate set of circumstances. Take the knowledge gained from the Exhibition, expand on it, and use it to become an informed participant in your own health care. This involves more than improving your diet or beginning a long overdue exercise program. It involves partnering with your doctor to understand what you—and your unique body—need to sustain a full and rewarding life.